How to become an IAM Engineer: Advanced level

James Relington

DEDICATION

This book is dedicated to all the professionals working tirelessly to secure digital systems and protect organizations from ever-evolving threats. To the cybersecurity teams, IT administrators, and identity management experts who ensure safe and seamless access for users—your work is invaluable. And to my family and friends, whose support and encouragement made this journey possible, thank you.

AKNOWLEDGEMENTS

I would like to express my deepest gratitude to everyone who contributed to the creation of this book. To my colleagues and mentors in the cybersecurity field, your insights and expertise have been invaluable. To the organizations and professionals who shared their experiences and best practices, your contributions have enriched this work. A special thank you to my family and friends for their unwavering support and encouragement throughout this journey. Finally, to the readers, thank you for your interest in identity lifecycle management—may this book help you navigate the evolving landscape of digital security with confidence.

IAM Protocol Internals: SAML Assertions, OAuth2 Flows, and OpenID Connect Claims

Identity and Access Management (IAM) relies on various protocols to facilitate secure authentication, authorization, and identity federation across applications and services. Among the most widely used protocols are Security Assertion Markup Language (SAML), OAuth 2.0, and OpenID Connect (OIDC). These protocols serve different purposes but often work together to enable seamless and secure identity transactions across distributed systems. Understanding the internal workings of these protocols is essential for IAM engineers who need to design and implement scalable, secure, and efficient identity solutions.

SAML is one of the oldest and most widely adopted standards for federated authentication. It is based on XML and allows identity providers (IdPs) to send authentication and authorization data to service providers (SPs) using digitally signed XML assertions. A SAML assertion is a structured token containing user authentication information, attribute statements, and authorization decisions. It is typically transported via HTTP POST or HTTP Redirect binding. SAML assertions have three primary components: authentication statements, attribute statements, and authorization decision statements. The authentication statement confirms that the user has been authenticated by the IdP and includes details such as authentication method and timestamp. The attribute statement carries user attributes, such as email, roles, or group memberships, which can be used by the SP to make access control decisions. The authorization decision statement indicates whether the user is allowed to perform specific actions within the SP's environment.

SAML uses a trust-based model where an IdP and an SP establish a trust relationship through public key cryptography. The IdP digitally signs the assertion using its private key, and the SP verifies the signature using the IdP's public key. This prevents tampering and ensures the integrity of the assertion. A key component of SAML authentication is the SAML Single Sign-On (SSO) flow, where a user authenticates once with the IdP and then gains access to multiple SPs without having to re-enter credentials. This reduces password fatigue and improves security by centralizing authentication at a trusted entity. However, SAML has limitations, including its reliance on XML, which can be cumbersome to parse, and its relative inefficiency compared to modern, lightweight protocols like OAuth 2.0 and OIDC.

OAuth 2.0 is a widely adopted authorization framework designed to allow third-party applications to access resources on behalf of a user without exposing their credentials. Unlike SAML, which primarily focuses on authentication, OAuth 2.0 is designed for delegated authorization. It provides a flexible and extensible model for granting limited access to protected resources via access tokens. OAuth 2.0 defines multiple grant types, including Authorization Code, Implicit, Resource Owner Password Credentials, and Client Credentials. The most secure and commonly used flow is the Authorization Code flow, which involves redirecting the user to an authorization server where they authenticate and approve the requested permissions. The authorization server then issues an authorization code, which the client exchanges for an access token. This ensures that access tokens are not exposed in the browser, reducing the risk of token leakage.

Access tokens in OAuth 2.0 are typically JSON Web Tokens (JWTs), which are compact, URL-safe, and digitally signed. JWTs contain claims that encode user information, scopes, and expiration times. They can be verified using public-private key cryptography, ensuring token integrity and preventing unauthorized modification. OAuth 2.0 also supports refresh tokens, which allow clients to obtain new access tokens without requiring the user to re-authenticate. This improves user experience and reduces the risk associated with long-lived access tokens. However, OAuth 2.0 alone does not provide authentication capabilities. It only grants access to resources but does not verify the user's identity. This gap is filled by OpenID Connect, an identity layer built on top of OAuth 2.0.

OpenID Connect (OIDC) extends OAuth 2.0 by introducing an ID token, which serves as a cryptographically verifiable proof of authentication. The ID token is also a JWT and includes claims that specify user identity information, authentication timestamps, and issuer details. One of the most important claims in an ID token is the "sub" (subject) claim, which uniquely identifies the authenticated user across different applications. Other claims include the "iss" (issuer) claim, which indicates the identity provider that issued the token, and the "aud" (audience) claim, which specifies the intended recipient of the token.

OIDC supports different authentication flows, including Authorization Code Flow, Implicit Flow, and Hybrid Flow. The Authorization Code Flow is the most secure and recommended approach, as it prevents tokens from being exposed to the user agent. In this flow, the client receives an authorization code from the authorization server and exchanges it for both an ID token and an access token. The Implicit Flow, while faster, is less secure because tokens are transmitted via URL fragments, making them susceptible to interception. The Hybrid Flow combines aspects of both Authorization Code and Implicit flows, providing additional flexibility for certain use cases.

One of the major advantages of OIDC is its ability to enable seamless SSO across applications and services. By leveraging ID tokens, applications can validate user identity without requiring separate authentication steps. This improves user experience while maintaining strong security controls. OIDC also supports dynamic client registration, enabling applications to register with an identity provider without manual configuration. This makes it easier to scale IAM solutions in dynamic environments.

IAM engineers need to understand the security considerations associated with these protocols. SAML, OAuth 2.0, and OIDC are susceptible to various attacks, including token replay attacks, token theft, and cross-site request forgery (CSRF). To mitigate these risks, engineers should implement best practices such as token expiration, audience validation, signature verification, and proper storage of refresh tokens. OAuth 2.0-based systems should use PKCE (Proof Key for Code Exchange) to prevent authorization code interception, while OIDC implementations should validate nonce values to prevent replay attacks.

Modern IAM solutions often combine these protocols to meet different security and interoperability requirements. Large enterprises and cloud service providers integrate SAML for legacy federated authentication, OAuth 2.0 for API authorization, and OIDC for modern authentication flows. By understanding the internals of these protocols, IAM engineers can design robust identity solutions that provide secure and seamless access across distributed systems. The ability to analyze, troubleshoot, and implement advanced security controls in these protocols is a fundamental skill for any IAM engineer working in large-scale environments.

Developing Custom Identity Providers (IdPs) and Service Providers (SPs)

Developing a custom Identity Provider (IdP) and Service Provider (SP) is a complex but crucial aspect of Identity and Access Management (IAM) engineering. Organizations often need to create custom IdPs to handle authentication and identity federation in a way that aligns with their security policies, compliance requirements, and unique infrastructure needs. Similarly, a custom SP must be capable of consuming identity assertions, validating authentication tokens, and enforcing access control mechanisms efficiently. A deep understanding of authentication protocols such as Security Assertion Markup Language (SAML), OAuth 2.0, and OpenID Connect (OIDC) is essential for implementing these systems successfully.

An Identity Provider (IdP) is responsible for authenticating users and issuing identity assertions that contain user attributes, authentication timestamps, and security tokens. These assertions are consumed by a Service Provider (SP), which grants or denies access based on the information received. A custom IdP must support various authentication mechanisms, such as password-based authentication, multi-factor authentication (MFA), biometric authentication, and federated authentication via social login providers or enterprise directories. To ensure high security, the IdP should support cryptographic signing of identity assertions using digital certificates and enforce strict authentication policies.

When developing a custom IdP, one of the first considerations is the choice of authentication protocol. SAML-based IdPs generate SAML assertions in XML format, which must be digitally signed and encrypted to prevent tampering and eavesdropping. Implementing a SAML IdP requires configuring metadata files, defining entity IDs, setting up key management strategies, and handling SAML binding methods such as HTTP-Redirect, HTTP-POST, and Artifact binding. The IdP must include a secure authentication backend, which can be a directory service like Active Directory (AD), Lightweight Directory Access Protocol (LDAP), or an external authentication service via RESTful APIs.

For modern authentication scenarios, an IdP should support OAuth 2.0 and OpenID Connect. OAuth 2.0 IdPs issue access tokens and refresh tokens to authorize clients without exposing user credentials. The IdP must include an authorization server capable of handling OAuth flows such as Authorization Code, Implicit, and Client Credentials Grant. It should also implement JSON Web Token (JWT) signing and validation using asymmetric cryptographic keys to ensure token integrity. OpenID Connect extends OAuth 2.0 by introducing an ID token, which is essential for authentication. The IdP should be able to generate ID tokens containing user claims such as "sub" (subject), "aud" (audience), and "iss" (issuer), and it must provide an endpoint for token introspection to allow resource servers to validate token authenticity.

A custom IdP should also support Single Sign-On (SSO) across multiple applications. This requires implementing session management and token revocation mechanisms. Security considerations such as cross-site request forgery (CSRF) protection, token expiration policies, and secure storage of refresh tokens are critical for preventing unauthorized access. Integrating an IdP with a SIEM (Security Information and Event Management) system is useful for monitoring authentication events, detecting anomalies, and responding to potential threats in real time.

On the other side, a Service Provider (SP) consumes authentication tokens from an IdP and grants access to users based on the received identity attributes. A custom SP must be capable of handling different assertion formats, including SAML assertions, OAuth 2.0 access tokens, and OIDC ID tokens. The SP must verify the digital signatures of these assertions to ensure their authenticity and prevent token forgery. In the case of SAML, this involves validating the XML signature using the public key of the IdP. For OAuth and OIDC, the SP must verify JWT signatures using the JSON Web Key Set (JWKS) endpoint provided by the IdP.

A robust SP implementation requires a flexible identity mapping mechanism. Users may authenticate via different IdPs, each providing varying attributes. The SP must be able to map these attributes to its internal identity store and determine user roles, permissions, and access levels dynamically. This is particularly important in environments where an SP integrates with multiple IdPs, such as in multi-cloud federations or B2B partnerships where users come from external organizations. The SP must enforce authorization policies using Role-Based Access Control (RBAC) or Attribute-Based Access Control (ABAC) and support dynamic authorization policies that adapt to real-time risk assessments.

Performance optimization is another crucial factor when developing custom IdPs and SPs. Token validation should be efficient, leveraging caching mechanisms to reduce cryptographic overhead. For instance, SPs can cache validated JWTs for a short period to avoid repeated signature verification on every request. Similarly, IdPs should optimize authentication workflows to minimize user friction while maintaining security. This includes supporting adaptive authentication, where additional security measures are enforced based on contextual factors such as geolocation, device reputation, or login patterns.

Developing a high-availability IdP or SP requires implementing failover strategies, database replication, and load balancing. IdPs should be designed to handle millions of authentication requests per second without introducing bottlenecks. This may involve deploying horizontally scalable authentication microservices, using in-memory session stores like Redis, and leveraging cloud-native technologies such as Kubernetes for auto-scaling. SPs must also implement mechanisms to gracefully handle IdP downtime, such as fallback authentication methods or federated identity chaining, where authentication can be rerouted to a secondary IdP if the primary one is unavailable.

Security is a paramount concern when developing IdPs and SPs. Threats such as replay attacks, token hijacking, and man-in-the-middle attacks must be mitigated through best practices like enforcing TLS for all identity transactions, implementing token binding to tie authentication tokens to specific client devices, and using signed and encrypted tokens to prevent unauthorized access. Advanced security features like device fingerprinting, AI-driven anomaly detection, and identity proofing should also be considered to enhance the security posture of the IdP.

In an enterprise setting, custom IdPs and SPs often need to integrate with other IAM components such as Identity Governance and Administration (IGA), Privileged Access Management (PAM), and endpoint security solutions. This allows organizations to enforce centralized identity policies, automate user provisioning and deprovisioning, and apply risk-based access controls. An IdP can be extended to support Just-In-Time (JIT) provisioning, where new users are dynamically created upon first authentication, reducing the administrative overhead of manually managing user accounts across multiple systems.

Custom IdP and SP implementations must also consider compliance with regulatory standards such as GDPR, HIPAA, and ISO 27001. Logging and auditing authentication events, enforcing strong password policies, and providing users with visibility into their authentication history are important measures for maintaining compliance. Implementing fine-grained consent management mechanisms, particularly in OIDC-based IdPs, ensures that users have control over how their identity information is shared across different applications.

A well-designed IdP and SP ecosystem enhances security, improves user experience, and enables seamless authentication across diverse applications. Organizations that require a high level of customization in their authentication and authorization workflows benefit significantly from building their own identity providers and service providers. By leveraging modern identity protocols, optimizing security measures, and implementing efficient authentication workflows, IAM engineers can develop IdPs and SPs that provide scalable, resilient, and future-proof identity solutions tailored to the organization's needs.

Advanced Federated Identity Management: Cross-Domain Trust and Security Considerations

Federated Identity Management (FIM) is a critical component of modern Identity and Access Management (IAM), enabling users to authenticate once and access multiple systems across different domains without needing separate credentials. In large enterprises, multi-cloud environments, and cross-organizational collaborations, advanced federated identity solutions provide seamless and secure authentication while reducing identity sprawl. The implementation of federated identity requires establishing a trust relationship between identity providers (IdPs) and service providers (SPs), handling authentication token exchanges securely, and mitigating risks associated with cross-domain identity propagation.

One of the core concepts of federated identity management is cross-domain trust, where an IdP in one domain asserts the identity of a user to an SP in another domain. This trust model must be carefully designed to prevent unauthorized access, identity spoofing, and privilege escalation. The trust between IdPs and SPs is typically established through cryptographic mechanisms such as digital signatures, certificate-based authentication, and JSON Web Key Sets (JWKS). The IdP signs authentication assertions, which the SP verifies before granting access. This ensures that identity claims cannot be tampered with during transmission and that authentication events originate from a trusted source.

To implement federated authentication, protocols such as Security Assertion Markup Language (SAML), OAuth 2.0, and OpenID Connect (OIDC) are commonly used. SAML-based federation is prevalent in enterprise settings where legacy applications require authentication via XML-based assertions. The SAML protocol enables IdPs to issue SAML assertions that contain authentication statements, attribute statements, and authorization decisions. These assertions are transmitted via SAML bindings such as HTTP-Redirect, HTTP-POST, or Artifact binding, depending on security and performance considerations. To enhance security, SAML assertions are signed using the IdP's private key and validated using the corresponding public key at the SP.

Modern federated identity implementations rely on OAuth 2.0 and OIDC, which offer more flexibility and security improvements over SAML. OAuth 2.0 provides delegated authorization by issuing access tokens that allow SPs to retrieve user information without exposing user credentials. OIDC extends OAuth 2.0 by introducing ID tokens, which serve as proof of authentication. These ID tokens contain claims about the authenticated user, such as the subject identifier (sub), issuer (iss), and audience (aud). The SP must validate these claims, ensuring that the token was issued by a trusted IdP, that it has not expired, and that it was intended for the specific application requesting authentication.

Cross-domain trust in federated identity requires managing trust anchors, certificate chains, and key rotation policies. In a multi-cloud or hybrid environment, organizations may need to establish federated authentication across cloud providers such as AWS, Azure, and Google Cloud, each with its own IAM system. Trust must be established between identity providers in different domains through metadata exchange, federation agreements, and mutual TLS authentication. This process involves configuring the IdP to trust certificates issued by the federation authority and ensuring that SPs validate assertions against an updated list of trusted IdPs.

One of the key security considerations in federated identity management is identity propagation and attribute mapping. When a user authenticates with an IdP, the identity attributes included in the assertion or token must be carefully mapped to the SP's authorization model. Different domains may use different attribute naming conventions, role structures, and permission models. Failure to properly map these attributes can result in privilege escalation, where a user receives higher privileges than intended. Organizations must implement attribute transformation policies, enforce strict role-based access control (RBAC) or attribute-based access control (ABAC) mechanisms, and apply least privilege principles.

Another critical aspect of federated identity security is token handling and lifecycle management. Access tokens and ID tokens must be protected against replay attacks, token theft, and misuse. OAuth 2.0 introduces token revocation and introspection mechanisms that allow SPs to verify token validity before granting access. Short-lived tokens with refresh token rotation can mitigate risks associated with token leakage. Additionally, the use of Proof Key for Code Exchange (PKCE) enhances security by preventing authorization code interception in OAuth 2.0 flows.

Federated identity solutions must also address the challenge of session management across domains. Since authentication happens at the IdP level, SPs rely on session tokens to maintain user sessions. If a user logs out from one SP, other federated services may still retain active sessions. Implementing Single Logout (SLO) mechanisms ensures that logout events propagate across all SPs in the federation. SAML supports front-channel and back-channel logout mechanisms, while OIDC provides logout endpoints to signal session termination across domains. Effective session management reduces the risk of session hijacking and unauthorized access after a user has logged out.

In addition to authentication and authorization security, federated identity must account for compliance and auditability. Enterprises operating in regulated industries such as finance, healthcare, and government must enforce strict access control policies, monitor authentication events, and maintain detailed audit logs. Centralized logging and monitoring solutions, integrated with SIEM platforms, enable real-time threat detection and response. Anomalous login behaviors, such as logins from unusual geolocations or impossible travel scenarios, can trigger risk-based authentication mechanisms, prompting additional verification steps.

Privacy considerations in federated identity management are also crucial. Users should have visibility into which SPs receive their identity attributes and consent mechanisms should be enforced where applicable. OIDC provides mechanisms for user consent and scope-based access control, ensuring that users grant explicit permissions before identity attributes are shared. Additionally, organizations should implement data minimization principles, only transmitting necessary attributes to SPs and anonymizing data where possible.

Scalability and high availability are fundamental for federated identity solutions in large enterprises and cloud environments. An IdP must be capable of handling millions of authentication requests per second while ensuring minimal latency. Load balancing, global traffic distribution, and redundant IdP deployments help maintain service availability. Federated identity architectures should be designed for failover, where alternative IdPs or backup authentication providers take over if the primary IdP becomes unavailable.

Advanced federated identity implementations extend beyond human authentication to support machine identities, APIs, and service-to-service authentication. Service accounts, non-human identities, and IoT devices require secure authentication mechanisms that align with federated identity principles. OAuth 2.0-based federated authentication enables secure API-to-API interactions using client credentials flow, while federated trust models in Kubernetes and service meshes provide identity federation between microservices.

Zero Trust principles have also influenced federated identity management, requiring continuous verification of identity assertions beyond initial authentication. Organizations are implementing continuous authentication mechanisms, integrating risk-based access policies, and leveraging AI-driven identity analytics to detect and respond to identity threats dynamically. Federated identity management in the Zero Trust era moves beyond traditional perimeter-based security models, ensuring that every authentication event is contextually evaluated based on user behavior, device security posture, and real-time threat intelligence.

The complexity of federated identity management grows as organizations expand their digital ecosystems, integrate multi-cloud infrastructures, and collaborate with external partners. Properly designing and securing cross-domain identity federations ensures seamless access, strong security, and compliance with global security standards. By leveraging the latest advancements in federated authentication protocols, enforcing robust access policies, and continuously monitoring authentication behaviors, organizations can maintain a scalable and resilient federated identity system that meets the evolving security demands of the digital landscape.

Protocol-Level Security: Attacks and Defenses in OAuth, SAML, and OIDC

Identity and Access Management (IAM) protocols such as OAuth 2.0, Security Assertion Markup Language (SAML), and OpenID Connect (OIDC) are essential components of modern authentication and authorization frameworks. These protocols enable secure identity federation, delegated authorization, and Single Sign-On (SSO) across applications. However, their widespread adoption makes them attractive targets for attackers who exploit protocol weaknesses, misconfigurations, and implementation flaws. Understanding the security threats at the protocol level and implementing proper defenses is crucial to safeguarding identity transactions from attacks such as token theft, replay attacks, signature forgery, and authorization bypass.

OAuth 2.0 is widely used for delegated authorization, allowing applications to access resources on behalf of users without exposing credentials. One of the most significant security risks in OAuth 2.0 is token leakage, where an attacker obtains an access token and uses it to access protected resources. This often occurs when tokens are transmitted over insecure channels or stored improperly in local storage or URL fragments. Attackers can intercept tokens using man-in-the-middle (MITM) attacks, browser-based vulnerabilities, or network sniffing techniques. To mitigate this, access tokens should always be transmitted over TLS-encrypted channels, and applications should use the Authorization Code flow with Proof Key for Code Exchange (PKCE) to prevent token interception. PKCE ensures that the authorization code exchanged between the client and authorization server is bound to a cryptographic verifier, reducing the risk of code interception attacks.

Another critical attack vector in OAuth 2.0 is token replay, where an attacker reuses a previously captured access token to gain unauthorized access. Since OAuth 2.0 access tokens are typically bearer tokens, they do not provide inherent protection against replay attacks. Implementing sender-constrained tokens using Mutual TLS (mTLS) or OAuth 2.0 Demonstrating Proof-of-Possession (DPoP) ensures that access tokens are tied to a specific client or session, preventing unauthorized reuse. Additionally, short-lived access tokens with refresh token rotation can limit the damage of stolen tokens by ensuring that they quickly expire and require re-authentication.

SAML, an XML-based authentication protocol widely used in enterprise environments, has its own set of security challenges. One of the most well-known attacks against SAML is XML Signature Wrapping (XSW), where an attacker modifies the structure of a signed SAML assertion to bypass authentication or authorization controls. This attack exploits weaknesses in how some implementations validate XML signatures, allowing attackers to insert malicious assertions without invalidating the original signature. Proper XML signature validation, including strict adherence to the XML Signature standard and canonicalization techniques, is essential to defending against this attack.

Another common vulnerability in SAML is the assertion replay attack. Since SAML assertions contain authentication information, a captured assertion can be reused by an attacker to gain access to a service provider without re-authentication. Implementing assertion expiration, one-time-use policies, and audience restrictions prevents assertion replay. Additionally, using signed and encrypted assertions ensures that only the intended recipient can read and validate the authentication data. Service providers should also validate the "NotBefore" and "NotOnOrAfter" timestamps in SAML assertions to prevent replay attacks.

OIDC, an authentication layer built on top of OAuth 2.0, introduces its own security considerations. One of the most significant threats in OIDC is ID token theft, where an attacker obtains a valid ID token and impersonates a user. Since ID tokens are often used for authentication, an attacker with a stolen token can gain unauthorized access to an application. To mitigate this, ID tokens should always be validated against the OpenID provider's JSON Web Key Set (JWKS) endpoint, ensuring that the token is properly signed and intended for the correct audience. Using audience and nonce validation helps prevent replay attacks by ensuring that tokens are not reused across different authentication sessions.

Another critical attack in OIDC is the mix-up attack, which occurs when an attacker tricks a client into sending authorization responses to the wrong OpenID provider. This is possible in multi-provider environments where a client supports multiple identity providers. The attacker manipulates the authorization flow to redirect responses to a rogue IdP, allowing them to capture authorization codes or ID tokens. The best defense against mix-up attacks is implementing provider validation, where the client verifies that the authorization server issuing the token matches the expected identity provider.

Authorization code injection attacks also pose a risk in OIDC and OAuth 2.0 flows. In this attack, an attacker intercepts an authorization code and injects it into an authorization response, tricking the client into exchanging the injected code for an access token. This allows the attacker to gain access to protected resources under the victim's identity. Enforcing PKCE in all authorization code flows mitigates this risk by ensuring that only clients with the correct code verifier can exchange an authorization code for tokens.

Cross-site request forgery (CSRF) is a common threat to OAuth 2.0, SAML, and OIDC implementations. CSRF attacks trick authenticated users into performing unwanted actions by exploiting their active sessions. Attackers craft malicious requests that are executed in the context of the victim's session, potentially authorizing unintended actions. CSRF defenses include requiring state parameters in OAuth and OIDC authorization requests, validating CSRF tokens in web applications, and implementing SameSite cookie attributes to prevent unauthorized cross-origin requests.

Token substitution attacks are another advanced threat in federated authentication scenarios. Attackers exploit weaknesses in how identity tokens are validated, replacing valid tokens with malicious ones issued by a different identity provider. Proper audience validation, signature verification, and issuer validation ensure that tokens are accepted only from trusted providers. Implementing a strict allowlist of authorized identity providers helps mitigate risks associated with rogue identity providers attempting to introduce fraudulent authentication tokens.

Implicit flow vulnerabilities remain a concern in OAuth 2.0 and OIDC. The implicit flow, historically used for browser-based applications, exposes access tokens in URL fragments, making them susceptible to leakage through browser history, referrer headers, and JavaScript injection attacks. Modern security best practices recommend avoiding implicit flow in favor of the Authorization Code flow with PKCE, which eliminates the need to expose tokens in URLs.

Session fixation attacks in federated authentication involve an attacker forcing a victim to use a predetermined session identifier, allowing the attacker to hijack the session after authentication. Implementing session binding techniques, where authentication sessions are tied to specific device attributes or IP addresses, reduces the risk of session fixation. Additionally, enforcing re-authentication for high-risk actions ensures that attackers cannot maintain unauthorized access even if they hijack a session.

As identity protocols evolve, attackers continuously develop new techniques to exploit weaknesses in authentication and authorization mechanisms. IAM engineers must stay ahead of emerging threats by implementing the latest security best practices, enforcing strict validation of identity assertions, and continuously monitoring authentication events for anomalies. Properly securing OAuth 2.0, SAML, and OIDC requires a multi-layered approach that includes cryptographic protections, strong session management, and rigorous validation of identity transactions. By understanding protocol-level security risks and implementing appropriate defenses, organizations can maintain robust and resilient identity systems that withstand modern attack techniques.

Advanced LDAP & Directory Services Optimization: Schema Design and Replication Strategies

Lightweight Directory Access Protocol (LDAP) and directory services form the backbone of identity and access management in enterprise environments. A well-optimized directory service ensures fast and reliable authentication, authorization, and identity resolution for applications, systems, and users across an organization. Advanced LDAP schema design and replication strategies play a crucial role in ensuring performance, scalability, and fault tolerance while maintaining security and compliance with regulatory frameworks. Understanding the intricacies of schema customization, indexing, and replication methodologies allows IAM engineers to build highly available and efficient directory services that meet the demands of modern infrastructure.

Schema design is one of the foundational aspects of LDAP directory services. A poorly designed schema can lead to inefficient queries, excessive disk usage, and degraded performance. LDAP directories store hierarchical identity data in a structured manner, using schema definitions that include object classes, attributes, and syntaxes. When extending or customizing an LDAP schema, it is essential to strike a balance between flexibility and standardization. Custom object classes should be designed to avoid unnecessary attribute duplication while maintaining compatibility with widely adopted schemas such as inetOrgPerson, posixAccount, and organizationalUnit.

One of the common challenges in schema design is defining attribute indexing strategies. LDAP directories rely on indexes to optimize search queries, reducing the time required to retrieve user records. Indexing strategies should be carefully planned based on query patterns and expected load. Common indexing types include equality indexes for exact match queries, substring indexes for partial matching, and presence indexes to optimize queries that check for attribute existence. Over-indexing can lead to increased memory and CPU consumption, while under-indexing can degrade query performance. Regular monitoring and tuning of indexing strategies ensure that the directory remains responsive under heavy workloads.

Another advanced consideration in LDAP schema design is the implementation of attribute inheritance and auxiliary object classes. Standard object classes may not always provide the necessary flexibility for complex directory structures. Auxiliary object classes allow attributes to be dynamically added to existing entries without modifying core object classes. This approach is beneficial when integrating directory services with multiple applications that require distinct sets of attributes without disrupting the overall schema integrity. Care must be taken to avoid excessive schema modifications, as frequent changes can lead to compatibility issues across applications relying on directory data.

Replication is a critical component of LDAP optimization, ensuring directory availability, fault tolerance, and load distribution. LDAP directories typically employ multi-master or master-slave replication models, each with distinct benefits and trade-offs. Multi-master replication allows multiple directory servers to handle write operations, improving redundancy and eliminating single points of failure. However, conflict resolution mechanisms must be implemented to handle cases where simultaneous writes occur on different replicas. Conflict resolution strategies often involve timestamp-based resolution, last-writer-wins policies, or custom reconciliation logic to maintain data consistency.

Master-slave replication, on the other hand, provides a simpler approach where a single master directory server handles write operations, and one or more read-only replicas distribute query loads. This model is effective for environments with high read traffic but limited write operations. Replication intervals should be optimized to strike a balance between performance and data consistency. Short replication intervals ensure rapid data synchronization but may introduce latency overhead, while longer intervals may lead to outdated directory entries in distributed environments.

LDAP replication security is another critical consideration. Replication traffic should always be encrypted using Transport Layer Security (TLS) to prevent unauthorized access or interception of sensitive identity data. Secure authentication mechanisms such as SASL (Simple Authentication and Security Layer) should be employed to validate replication peers before allowing data synchronization. Additionally, access controls should be enforced to restrict replication access to trusted servers, minimizing the risk of unauthorized modifications or data leaks.

Performance tuning of directory services also involves connection handling and caching strategies. LDAP servers must be optimized to handle concurrent connections efficiently, ensuring that authentication and search requests are processed without bottlenecks. Connection pooling techniques, where directory-aware applications maintain persistent LDAP connections instead of repeatedly establishing new ones, significantly reduce authentication latency and improve overall system performance.

Caching mechanisms further enhance LDAP performance by reducing the number of direct queries to directory backends. Directory servers can implement in-memory caches for frequently accessed attributes, reducing disk I/O and query response times. Client-side caching, where applications store LDAP query results for short durations, further alleviates load on the directory server. Cache invalidation strategies must be carefully designed to ensure that cached data does not become stale, leading to inconsistencies in authentication and authorization workflows.

In large-scale environments, LDAP partitioning and load balancing techniques improve scalability and resilience. Directory partitions allow different subsets of directory data to be stored across multiple servers, reducing the query load on individual nodes. Partitioning is particularly useful in global deployments where directory data is logically divided by geographic regions, organizational units, or business functions. Load balancing techniques such as DNS-based round-robin, reverse proxy configurations, or dedicated LDAP load balancers distribute query traffic efficiently across multiple directory replicas.

Another optimization strategy for LDAP-based identity management involves attribute-based access controls (ABAC). By implementing fine-grained access control policies, directory administrators can enforce restrictions based on attributes such as department, job role, or geographic location. Modern directory services support dynamic policy enforcement using attribute filters, ensuring that access rights are evaluated in real-time based on directory data. Implementing ABAC within LDAP directories strengthens security postures by limiting access to sensitive information while maintaining flexibility for dynamic access scenarios.

Directory health monitoring and log analysis are essential for proactive maintenance and threat detection. LDAP logs provide valuable insights into authentication failures, excessive query loads, and potential brute-force attacks. Regular log reviews enable administrators to identify unusual patterns and respond to security threats before they escalate. Integrating LDAP logs with SIEM (Security Information and Event Management) platforms enhances visibility into identity-related security events, enabling automated threat detection and incident response.

Disaster recovery planning for directory services ensures business continuity in the event of server failures or data corruption. Backup strategies should include both full directory snapshots and incremental backups to minimize data loss. Replication-based recovery models provide an additional layer of redundancy, allowing standby directory servers to take over operations in case of primary server failures. Automated failover mechanisms, combined with health checks and monitoring alerts, enable rapid recovery with minimal disruption to authentication services.

As directory services continue to evolve, modern architectures integrate cloud-based identity providers with traditional LDAP directories. Hybrid identity models leverage cloud identity platforms such as Microsoft Entra ID, Okta, and Google Cloud Identity to extend authentication and authorization capabilities beyond on-premise LDAP deployments. Secure synchronization mechanisms, such as SCIM (System for Cross-domain Identity Management), facilitate seamless identity updates between cloud and on-premise directories. Hybrid approaches enable organizations to maintain legacy LDAP-based authentication while transitioning to modern identity federation solutions.

LDAP and directory services remain a cornerstone of enterprise IAM strategies, providing centralized identity storage, authentication, and access management. By implementing advanced schema design principles, optimizing replication strategies, and enhancing security mechanisms, IAM engineers can build scalable and resilient directory infrastructures. Continuous monitoring, performance tuning, and integration with cloud identity services ensure that LDAP directories remain efficient, secure, and adaptable to the evolving demands of modern identity ecosystems.

Building Custom IAM Connectors: API, SCIM, and Custom Provisioning Flows

Identity and Access Management (IAM) solutions often need to integrate with various enterprise applications, cloud services, and legacy systems. To achieve seamless identity provisioning, synchronization, and lifecycle management, organizations rely on IAM connectors—custom-built integrations that allow IAM platforms to communicate with external identity stores and applications. While many commercial IAM solutions provide out-of-the-box connectors, building custom IAM connectors is often necessary to support unique business logic, legacy systems, or proprietary applications. Developing robust IAM connectors requires a deep understanding of API interactions, the System for Cross-domain Identity Management (SCIM) standard, and advanced provisioning workflows that ensure data consistency and security.

Custom IAM connectors primarily facilitate user provisioning, deprovisioning, role assignment, and entitlement management across disparate systems. These connectors must efficiently handle CRUD (Create, Read, Update, Delete) operations for identities while maintaining synchronization with the central IAM system. APIs play a crucial role in connector development, allowing IAM platforms to interact with external systems in real time. Many modern applications expose RESTful or GraphQL APIs that enable identity management operations, while legacy applications may still rely on SOAP-based web services or direct database interactions. A well-designed IAM connector must abstract these complexities, providing a standardized way for the IAM system to manage identities without requiring deep customization for each target system.

One of the key challenges in building custom IAM connectors is handling authentication and authorization when communicating with external APIs. OAuth 2.0 is the most common authorization framework for API-based integrations, requiring connectors to manage access tokens securely. In cases where APIs do not support OAuth, IAM connectors may need to rely on API keys, mutual TLS authentication, or client certificates. Proper token management, including secure storage of credentials and automatic token refresh mechanisms, is critical to preventing unauthorized access and ensuring high availability of identity provisioning services.

SCIM (System for Cross-domain Identity Management) is an open standard that simplifies identity provisioning by providing a standardized API for managing user accounts and groups. SCIM enables interoperability between IAM systems and external applications, reducing the complexity of building custom connectors. A SCIM-compliant IAM connector leverages RESTful endpoints to create, update, and delete user identities in a consistent format. SCIM uses JSON-based payloads, making it efficient and easy to integrate with modern cloud applications. When developing a SCIM connector, it is essential to implement schema mapping to align SCIM attributes with the target system's data model. This involves translating SCIM attributes such as userName, emails, and groups into the corresponding attributes used by the target application.

SCIM also supports bulk operations, which are useful for synchronizing large identity datasets. A well-optimized SCIM connector should handle batch processing efficiently, ensuring that bulk updates do not overload the target system. Additionally, SCIM provides event-driven provisioning through the PATCH method, allowing IAM systems to update only modified attributes instead of re-provisioning entire user objects. Implementing SCIM pagination and filtering mechanisms improves performance by enabling incremental data retrieval instead of full directory synchronization.

For applications that do not support SCIM natively, custom provisioning flows must be developed to bridge the gap between the IAM system and the target application. Custom provisioning logic often involves workflow automation, where identity changes trigger specific actions such as account creation, group membership updates, or attribute synchronization. These workflows can be implemented using IAM orchestration tools, event-driven architectures, or direct database updates. A robust provisioning flow must include retry logic, failure handling, and transaction rollbacks to ensure consistency, especially when dealing with distributed systems.

Event-driven identity provisioning is an advanced approach that improves efficiency by eliminating periodic batch processing. Instead of relying on scheduled sync jobs, event-driven IAM connectors listen for real-time changes in the identity store and immediately propagate updates to downstream applications. This can be achieved using message queues, event streaming platforms like Apache Kafka, or webhook-based notifications. For example, when a user is onboarded in the HR system, an event is published that triggers the IAM connector to provision the user account in all required applications.

Deprovisioning is a critical aspect of IAM connector development, ensuring that user accounts are disabled or deleted when an employee leaves the organization or an access request is revoked. Improper deprovisioning can lead to orphaned accounts, which pose significant security risks. IAM connectors must support configurable deprovisioning policies, including soft deletion (disabling accounts without removing them) and hard deletion (permanent removal of accounts and associated entitlements). Additionally, IAM connectors should enforce role-based deprovisioning, where only specific entitlements are revoked based on changes in user roles or access policies.

Security considerations in IAM connector development go beyond API authentication. Connectors must implement data encryption for sensitive identity attributes, enforce least privilege access when interacting with external systems, and validate input data to prevent injection attacks. Logging and auditing capabilities are essential for tracking identity transactions, providing visibility into provisioning activities, and ensuring compliance with security policies. Secure logging practices should include masking of personally identifiable information (PII) while preserving enough detail for troubleshooting and forensic analysis.

Scalability is another key factor in IAM connector performance. As organizations grow, IAM connectors must handle increasing volumes of identity transactions without degrading performance. Load balancing and horizontal scaling strategies should be implemented to distribute provisioning workloads across multiple instances of the IAM connector. Caching mechanisms, such as in-memory attribute caching, reduce redundant API calls and improve response times. Optimized database queries and efficient schema indexing further enhance performance when IAM connectors interact with relational or NoSQL databases.

Hybrid IAM environments, where organizations use a mix of on-premises and cloud-based identity systems, require connectors that bridge both worlds. Legacy applications often lack modern identity APIs, necessitating custom connectors that interact with directory services like Active Directory (AD), LDAP-based directories, or proprietary IAM platforms. These connectors must translate cloud-native identity attributes into legacy identity models while ensuring bidirectional synchronization between cloud IAM systems and on-premise directories.

Extensibility is an important design principle when building IAM connectors. A well-architected connector should be modular and configurable, allowing administrators to adapt it to different applications without modifying core code. Using plugin-based architectures, policy-driven provisioning engines, and declarative configuration files enables IAM connectors to support a wide range of applications with minimal customization.

Custom IAM connector development requires a comprehensive approach that considers API security, standardization through SCIM, real-time event-driven provisioning, and robust deprovisioning mechanisms. By leveraging best practices in identity synchronization, security hardening, and performance optimization, IAM engineers can build scalable and resilient IAM connectors that seamlessly integrate with diverse enterprise applications and cloud services.

Privileged Access Management (PAM) Hardening and Zero Standing Privileges (ZSP)

Privileged Access Management (PAM) is a critical component of enterprise security, designed to protect highly sensitive accounts and access to critical systems. These privileged accounts, including administrator, root, and service accounts, have elevated permissions that can be exploited if compromised. Traditional PAM strategies focus on securing and managing these accounts, but modern security paradigms demand stricter controls, particularly in high-risk environments where persistent privileged access represents an unnecessary attack surface. This has led to the adoption of Zero Standing Privileges (ZSP), a security principle that eliminates permanently assigned privileged access in favor of Just-In-Time (JIT) access models.

A well-hardened PAM system enforces strict access control policies, ensuring that privileged accounts are used only when necessary and in a highly controlled manner. The first step in hardening PAM is eliminating shared accounts and enforcing individual accountability. Every privileged action should be associated with a specific user, reducing the risk of unauthorized activities going unnoticed. This requires the implementation of unique, dynamically assigned privileged credentials that expire after use. Password vaulting and rotation mechanisms ensure that static credentials are never reused or exposed. Modern PAM solutions automatically rotate passwords and API keys, preventing attackers from leveraging stolen credentials.

Role-Based Access Control (RBAC) and Attribute-Based Access Control (ABAC) play a key role in PAM hardening. Instead of providing blanket administrative privileges, access should be granted based on specific tasks and dynamically adjusted according to contextual factors. For example, an engineer requiring access to a production database should only be granted that privilege for a predefined period and under specific conditions, such as approval from a manager or authentication via multi-factor authentication (MFA). Implementing dynamic access policies that adapt to user behavior, risk scores, and system health further strengthens PAM defenses.

Session monitoring and recording provide additional layers of security by allowing security teams to track and audit privileged activities in real-time. PAM solutions should integrate with Security Information and Event Management (SIEM) platforms to detect anomalies, such as unauthorized command execution, privilege escalation attempts, and access outside of approved time windows. Advanced behavioral analytics can be applied to PAM logs to identify potential insider threats or compromised accounts before they result in data breaches.

The Zero Standing Privileges (ZSP) model goes beyond traditional PAM by eliminating the concept of always-available privileged accounts. Under ZSP, no user has persistent administrative privileges; instead, access is granted dynamically based on business needs. Just-In-Time (JIT) access mechanisms ensure that users receive privileged access only when required, and only for the duration of their task. This reduces the attack surface by limiting the time window in which an attacker could exploit elevated privileges.

Implementing ZSP requires a combination of ephemeral accounts, privilege elevation workflows, and time-restricted access. Ephemeral accounts are temporary privileged accounts created on demand and destroyed after use. These accounts do not persist beyond the duration of the session, making them highly resistant to compromise. Privilege elevation workflows enforce approval processes, requiring users to justify access requests and obtain validation from security teams before privileges are granted. Time-restricted access further limits exposure by ensuring that elevated privileges automatically expire, reducing the likelihood of privilege abuse.

A key challenge in implementing ZSP is ensuring seamless operational workflows without introducing excessive friction. Automation plays a crucial role in achieving this balance. Self-service privilege requests integrated with Identity Governance and Administration (IGA) systems allow users to request access via automated workflows that enforce policy-driven approvals. Machine learning-based risk assessments can be integrated to determine whether a request should be auto-approved or require additional scrutiny. For example, a low-risk request from a known device in a corporate network might be granted automatically, whereas a request from an unfamiliar location or device might trigger additional verification steps.

Infrastructure and cloud environments pose unique challenges for PAM and ZSP implementations. In hybrid and multi-cloud environments, privileged access extends beyond traditional user accounts to include API keys, cloud service roles, and infrastructure-as-code automation tools. Cloud-native PAM solutions must enforce least privilege principles across cloud workloads, ensuring that IAM roles, service accounts, and automation scripts do not retain excessive permissions. Cloud access policies should be dynamically scoped, allowing only the minimum necessary permissions based on workload context and real-time activity monitoring.

DevOps and CI/CD pipelines introduce another layer of complexity, as developers and automation tools frequently require elevated access to deploy code, modify configurations, and manage infrastructure. Implementing ZSP in DevOps environments involves integrating PAM solutions with secrets management tools such as HashiCorp Vault, AWS Secrets Manager, or Azure Key Vault. Instead of hardcoding credentials in scripts or CI/CD pipelines, these secrets should be dynamically retrieved from a secure vault at runtime. Additionally, ephemeral credentials should be used for infrastructure access, ensuring that no long-lived credentials are stored in code repositories or exposed in logs.

Service accounts and machine identities require special consideration in PAM and ZSP models. Unlike human users, service accounts often need persistent access to perform automated tasks. However, static credentials for service accounts represent a significant security risk if not properly managed. To mitigate this risk, service accounts should be assigned only the necessary permissions, and their credentials should be regularly rotated or replaced with certificate-based authentication. Where possible, workload identities should be leveraged instead of traditional service accounts, allowing applications to authenticate using temporary credentials issued by cloud IAM providers.

Implementing ZSP also requires cultural and process changes within an organization. Security teams must educate users on the importance of temporary access and ensure that IT operations, development teams, and administrators understand the benefits of Just-In-Time privilege elevation. Resistance to change is common, particularly among teams accustomed to having persistent administrator privileges. To encourage adoption, PAM solutions should be designed with usability in mind, minimizing operational disruptions while maintaining strong security controls.

Incident response and forensic analysis benefit significantly from PAM hardening and ZSP models. Since privileged actions are tightly controlled and monitored, security teams can quickly trace any unauthorized or suspicious activities to their source. Automated incident response workflows can be triggered based on anomaly detection, immediately revoking elevated privileges and isolating compromised accounts. Integrating PAM with endpoint detection and response (EDR) tools enhances the ability to contain and mitigate security threats in real time.

Regulatory compliance frameworks increasingly emphasize privileged access control as a critical security requirement. Standards such as NIST 800-53, ISO 27001, and GDPR mandate strict access controls, auditability, and least privilege enforcement for privileged accounts. By implementing PAM hardening strategies and ZSP models, organizations can meet compliance requirements while reducing the risk of privileged account misuse, insider threats, and external attacks.

The evolution of privileged access security requires organizations to shift from traditional, static privilege models to dynamic, risk-aware access strategies. By eliminating standing privileges, enforcing Just-In-Time access, and continuously monitoring privileged activities, enterprises can significantly reduce their attack surface and enhance their overall security posture. PAM hardening combined with ZSP represents the next generation of privileged access security, ensuring that sensitive credentials and privileged operations remain tightly controlled, dynamically allocated, and continuously protected from emerging threats.

Writing Secure IAM APIs: JWT Security, OAuth Introspection, and Token Revocation

Identity and Access Management (IAM) APIs are at the core of modern authentication and authorization frameworks, enabling secure interactions between users, applications, and services. To ensure robust security, IAM APIs must implement strong token management, prevent unauthorized access, and mitigate risks associated with token forgery, leakage, and abuse. JSON Web Tokens (JWTs) serve as the primary mechanism for conveying identity and access credentials in modern IAM systems, often used in conjunction with OAuth 2.0 and

OpenID Connect (OIDC) to manage authentication and authorization. While JWTs provide flexibility and efficiency, their security depends on proper signing, validation, storage, and expiration controls. In addition, OAuth introspection and token revocation mechanisms play a crucial role in preventing unauthorized access and ensuring real-time access control.

JWTs are compact, URL-safe tokens that encode user claims and access rights, typically signed using HMAC (HS256) or asymmetric cryptographic algorithms such as RSA (RS256) and ECDSA (ES256). A secure IAM API must enforce strict validation of JWTs, including signature verification, issuer and audience validation, and expiration checks. If JWT validation is improperly implemented, attackers can forge or manipulate tokens to gain unauthorized access. The public key used for verifying JWT signatures should be securely distributed via a JSON Web Key Set (JWKS) endpoint, allowing services to dynamically fetch and validate token signatures without manual configuration.

One of the most common security pitfalls in JWT implementation is allowing excessively long-lived tokens. A JWT should have a short expiration time (exp claim) to minimize the impact of a compromised token. While refresh tokens can be used to obtain new JWTs, they must be stored securely and rotated periodically to prevent misuse. Access tokens should always be bound to specific audiences (aud claim), ensuring they cannot be reused across unintended applications. Including a unique identifier (jti claim) in JWTs enables token tracking and revocation, helping prevent token replay attacks.

Storing JWTs securely is critical to preventing token theft. Tokens should never be stored in browser local storage, as this makes them susceptible to cross-site scripting (XSS) attacks. Instead, HTTP-only secure cookies should be used for web-based applications, preventing JavaScript access to tokens while ensuring they are transmitted only over HTTPS. In mobile and backend applications, tokens should be stored in secure, encrypted storage environments such as the iOS Keychain or Android Keystore. Additionally, IAM APIs should enforce token binding techniques, such as OAuth 2.0 Proof of Possession (DPoP), to tie tokens to specific clients and prevent misuse by unauthorized actors.

OAuth 2.0 token introspection enhances security by allowing APIs to validate the status of an access token in real time. Unlike JWTs, which are self-contained and do not require an external lookup, introspection queries an authorization server to verify whether a token is active, expired, or revoked. This is particularly useful in scenarios where token revocation is needed, as it enables APIs to reject tokens that have been explicitly invalidated. Secure IAM APIs should implement introspection endpoints using mutual TLS (mTLS) or OAuth client authentication to prevent unauthorized token validation requests. Introspection responses should include metadata such as the token's scope, client ID, and user ID, allowing APIs to enforce fine-grained access control based on real-time token status.

Token revocation is a critical security feature that allows administrators and users to invalidate access tokens and refresh tokens when needed. In OAuth 2.0, refresh token revocation is particularly important, as refresh tokens provide long-term access and can be exploited if compromised. Secure IAM APIs must implement OAuth 2.0's token revocation endpoint, ensuring that compromised tokens cannot be reused. When a refresh token is revoked, all associated access tokens should also be invalidated to prevent unauthorized access. Blacklisting revoked tokens in a centralized token store or maintaining a token blocklist in a high-performance cache such as Redis enables APIs to enforce revocation efficiently.

To further enhance security, IAM APIs should support authorization policies based on risk assessments. Continuous authentication mechanisms can analyze user behavior, device posture, and geolocation data to determine whether a token should be revoked or revalidated. If an anomaly is detected, such as an access token being used from an unusual location or a high-risk IP address, IAM APIs should trigger additional authentication steps or revoke the token in real time.

OAuth 2.0 scopes and claims provide another layer of access control, ensuring that access tokens grant only the necessary permissions required for a specific operation. IAM APIs must validate the scopes associated with each token and enforce least privilege access, preventing over-permissioned tokens from being exploited. Dynamic scope enforcement allows IAM systems to adjust token permissions based on contextual factors, reducing the risk of privilege escalation.

Logging and auditing play a crucial role in IAM API security, providing visibility into authentication and authorization events. IAM APIs should log token issuance, refresh events, introspection requests, and revocation actions to detect anomalies and facilitate forensic investigations. Logs should be stored in a secure, tamper-proof environment and integrated with Security Information and Event Management (SIEM) platforms for real-time monitoring and alerting. Implementing structured logging formats, such as JSON-based logs, enables efficient analysis and correlation of security events.

Performance optimization is another important consideration when securing IAM APIs. While JWT validation is fast due to its stateless nature, frequent token introspection and revocation checks can introduce latency. IAM APIs should implement caching strategies for introspection responses, reducing the load on authorization servers while ensuring real-time access control. Additionally, rate limiting and API throttling mechanisms should be enforced to prevent token enumeration attacks, where attackers attempt to guess or brute-force valid access tokens.

Federated identity scenarios introduce additional security challenges in IAM APIs. When integrating with external identity providers (IdPs) using OpenID Connect, IAM APIs must validate ID tokens against the IdP's JWKS endpoint and enforce strict audience and issuer validation. Cross-domain trust should be carefully managed, ensuring that tokens issued by third-party IdPs are only accepted for explicitly approved use cases. Hybrid identity models, where IAM APIs interact with both cloud and on-premise identity providers, require additional safeguards, such as token translation gateways and secure session management.

Secure IAM APIs must also address potential vulnerabilities in OAuth 2.0 authorization flows. Implementing Proof Key for Code Exchange (PKCE) prevents authorization code interception attacks by ensuring that the authorization code cannot be reused by an attacker. Additionally, IAM APIs should enforce state parameter validation in

OAuth authorization requests, mitigating the risk of cross-site request forgery (CSRF) attacks.

Zero Trust principles reinforce the need for continuous validation of access tokens, moving beyond static authentication events. IAM APIs should adopt adaptive access control models that dynamically adjust token lifetimes, scope permissions, and revocation rules based on risk signals. Integrating IAM APIs with modern security frameworks, such as Cloud-Native Application Protection Platforms (CNAPP) and Extended Detection and Response (XDR), ensures that authentication and authorization processes align with evolving threat landscapes.

By implementing robust JWT security measures, enforcing OAuth introspection and token revocation policies, and adopting continuous authentication models, IAM APIs can provide strong identity assurance while minimizing security risks. As IAM ecosystems continue to evolve, API security remains a foundational element in protecting digital identities, securing access to critical resources, and preventing unauthorized transactions across distributed applications and cloud environments.

Implementing Secure REST and GraphQL APIs for Identity and Access Management

Identity and Access Management (IAM) solutions rely heavily on APIs to facilitate authentication, authorization, and identity lifecycle management. Secure API implementation is essential to prevent unauthorized access, mitigate security risks, and ensure compliance with best practices. REST and GraphQL APIs play a fundamental role in IAM systems by enabling identity providers (IdPs), service providers (SPs), and applications to communicate securely. While REST APIs follow a traditional request-response model, GraphQL APIs provide more flexibility by allowing clients to query specific identity attributes dynamically. Regardless of the architectural choice, securing IAM APIs requires strict access controls, proper authentication mechanisms, data protection strategies, and mitigation of common API vulnerabilities.

REST APIs in IAM systems typically expose endpoints for user authentication, token issuance, role-based access control (RBAC), identity federation, and audit logging. Secure REST API design begins with enforcing strong authentication mechanisms, such as OAuth 2.0 authorization flows or OpenID Connect (OIDC) authentication tokens. All requests to REST endpoints must require authentication, ensuring that only authorized clients can interact with IAM resources. JSON Web Tokens (JWTs) are commonly used for securing REST APIs, allowing stateless authentication and reducing the overhead associated with session management. However, JWTs must be validated correctly, checking signatures, expiration times, and issuer claims before granting access to protected resources.

Access control in REST APIs should follow the principle of least privilege, ensuring that API consumers can only perform actions necessary for their role. Role-based and attribute-based access control mechanisms should be enforced at the API gateway level, limiting access to identity attributes, provisioning actions, and administrative endpoints. Fine-grained access controls allow security teams to define API policies that restrict access based on user identity, device posture, geolocation, or risk scores. Implementing scopes in OAuth 2.0 authorization tokens helps enforce granular access controls by allowing APIs to validate whether a client has the necessary permissions to execute a request.

One of the most common vulnerabilities in IAM REST APIs is inadequate protection of sensitive data. Identity-related APIs often return personally identifiable information (PII), such as email addresses, phone numbers, and authentication logs. To mitigate the risk of data exposure, REST APIs must implement output filtering and data masking techniques, ensuring that only authorized consumers can access sensitive identity attributes. Enforcing encryption in transit using TLS 1.2 or higher is mandatory to prevent man-in-the-middle (MITM) attacks. Additionally, API responses should never include sensitive data in URL parameters or query strings, as they can be logged in browser history or intercepted by malicious actors.

Rate limiting and request throttling are critical to preventing API abuse and denial-of-service (DoS) attacks in IAM systems. Implementing rate-limiting strategies ensures that API consumers cannot overwhelm authentication and authorization services with excessive requests. API gateways should enforce per-user, per-application, or per-IP rate limits, dynamically adjusting thresholds based on observed traffic patterns. Adaptive rate limiting, combined with anomaly detection, allows IAM APIs to block abusive clients while maintaining availability for legitimate users.

GraphQL APIs introduce unique security challenges due to their flexible query structure. Unlike REST APIs, which expose predefined endpoints, GraphQL allows clients to request arbitrary data structures, potentially leading to excessive data exposure if not properly controlled. Securing GraphQL APIs for IAM requires enforcing strict query validation, preventing users from querying unauthorized identity attributes. Implementing query depth limiting and complexity analysis ensures that GraphQL requests do not overload IAM backends with expensive operations, reducing the risk of GraphQL denial-of-service (DoS) attacks.

Authentication in GraphQL APIs follows similar principles as REST, requiring OAuth 2.0, OIDC, or API key-based authentication to access identity-related queries and mutations. Role-based access control (RBAC) and attribute-based access control (ABAC) must be integrated into GraphQL resolvers, ensuring that users can only access data permitted by their roles. Field-level authorization policies should be enforced within resolvers, allowing fine-grained access control to user attributes. For example, an IAM GraphQL API should restrict access to administrative attributes such as group memberships and privileged roles based on the caller's identity.

Preventing excessive data retrieval is a major concern in IAM GraphQL implementations. Unlike REST, where API designers define response structures, GraphQL clients dictate what data is returned. This flexibility can lead to over-fetching, where clients inadvertently or maliciously retrieve large amounts of identity data in a single request. Implementing introspection controls, query complexity scoring, and response size limits ensures that GraphQL APIs do not expose excessive user information. Rate limiting at the query level further prevents clients from executing expensive queries that impact API performance.

Token security is critical for both REST and GraphQL IAM APIs. Access tokens and ID tokens must be validated on every request, ensuring they have not expired or been revoked. OAuth 2.0 token introspection endpoints allow APIs to verify token validity in real-time, reducing the risk of token replay attacks. Token revocation mechanisms should be enforced to immediately invalidate compromised or misused tokens, preventing unauthorized API access. For long-lived sessions, refresh tokens should be rotated periodically, ensuring that persistent access does not rely on a single token instance.

Logging and monitoring play a crucial role in IAM API security, providing visibility into authentication attempts, API access patterns, and potential security threats. IAM APIs should generate structured logs capturing authentication failures, authorization violations, and anomalous access requests. Logs should be securely transmitted to centralized security information and event management (SIEM) platforms for real-time analysis. Implementing anomaly detection and behavioral analytics on API logs helps identify malicious activities, such as token reuse, brute-force authentication attempts, and unauthorized API enumeration.

To enhance security further, IAM APIs should integrate with Web Application Firewalls (WAFs) and API gateways, providing an additional layer of protection against common threats such as injection attacks, broken authentication, and API scraping. API security gateways enable centralized policy enforcement, allowing IAM teams to implement authentication, authorization, and traffic filtering rules consistently across all IAM endpoints.

Multi-tenancy introduces additional challenges for securing IAM APIs. In environments where multiple organizations or business units share a single IAM instance, APIs must enforce strict tenant isolation to prevent data leakage. Tenant-aware access controls ensure that users and applications can only interact with identities and resources belonging to their organization. Secure multi-tenancy implementations prevent cross-tenant identity lookups, ensuring that IAM APIs do not expose unauthorized identity information.

As organizations adopt microservices architectures, IAM APIs must support secure service-to-service authentication. Mutual TLS (mTLS) and OAuth 2.0 client credentials grant flows enable secure authentication between microservices, ensuring that IAM requests are only processed by trusted components. API gateways should enforce mutual authentication policies, preventing unauthorized services from interacting with IAM endpoints.

Secure IAM API development requires a combination of authentication best practices, access control enforcement, data protection mechanisms, and threat mitigation strategies. Whether implementing REST or GraphQL APIs, IAM engineers must adopt a defense-in-depth approach, ensuring that authentication tokens are securely managed, API requests are properly authorized, and sensitive identity data remains protected from unauthorized access. By continuously monitoring for emerging threats and refining security policies, IAM APIs can provide strong identity assurance while minimizing security risks.

Developing Policy Engines for Dynamic Authorization using XACML and Open Policy Agent (OPA)

Dynamic authorization is a critical component of modern Identity and Access Management (IAM), enabling fine-grained, context-aware access control decisions that go beyond traditional Role-Based Access Control (RBAC) models. As organizations adopt complex security architectures across cloud, hybrid, and on-premises environments, enforcing access policies dynamically requires robust policy engines capable of evaluating user attributes, environmental conditions, and application-specific rules in real time. Extensible Access Control Markup Language (XACML) and Open Policy Agent (OPA) are two powerful policy frameworks that provide a flexible and scalable approach to dynamic authorization. Implementing a policy engine based on these technologies enhances security by enforcing precise access control decisions across microservices, APIs, and enterprise applications.

XACML is an industry-standard access control language designed to define, enforce, and manage authorization policies in a structured and standardized manner. XACML operates based on the principles of Attribute-Based Access Control (ABAC), where access decisions are determined by evaluating attributes such as user roles, resource types, request context, and environmental conditions. An XACML-based policy engine consists of multiple components, including the Policy Enforcement Point (PEP), Policy Decision Point (PDP), Policy Administration Point (PAP), and Policy Information Point (PIP). The PEP intercepts access requests and forwards them to the PDP, which evaluates policies based on rules defined in the PAP and retrieves additional data from the PIP when necessary.

One of the key advantages of XACML is its ability to handle complex authorization scenarios that involve hierarchical permissions, conditional access rules, and delegation of privileges. Policies in XACML are expressed using XML-based syntax, defining rules such as "only managers can approve financial transactions above $10,000" or "access to customer records is restricted based on geographic location." The policy evaluation process relies on combining multiple rules using effect-based decision strategies, such as deny-overrides, permit-overrides, or first-applicable policies.

To implement an XACML-based policy engine, organizations must deploy a PDP that can process policy requests and return authorization decisions to the PEP. Open-source XACML implementations, such as WSO2 Identity Server and Balana, provide reference implementations that integrate with IAM platforms and applications. Custom XACML engines can be developed by implementing the XACML Request/Response interface, allowing organizations to extend policy evaluation capabilities with custom attributes, external data sources, and integration with enterprise directories. Performance optimization in XACML policy engines involves caching policy evaluations, preloading frequently accessed policies, and distributing policy decision points across multiple nodes to handle high-throughput authorization requests.

While XACML provides a structured approach to dynamic authorization, its XML-based syntax and complexity can be challenging to manage in modern cloud-native environments. Open Policy Agent (OPA) has emerged as a lightweight, highly scalable alternative for implementing policy-driven authorization across distributed systems. OPA is a general-purpose policy engine designed for microservices, Kubernetes, API gateways, and service meshes. Unlike XACML, which relies on XML policies, OPA uses Rego, a declarative policy language optimized for flexibility and performance.

OPA operates as a standalone decision engine that evaluates policies against input data and returns boolean decisions or structured responses. Policies in OPA are stored as JSON documents, making them easier to integrate with modern applications and infrastructure components. A typical OPA policy might define rules such as "users can access an API endpoint only if they have the appropriate role and IP address within an allowed range" or "Kubernetes workloads should not have privileged container permissions unless explicitly approved." These policies are evaluated dynamically at runtime, ensuring that authorization decisions reflect the latest security requirements and compliance mandates.

To integrate OPA into an IAM architecture, organizations deploy OPA agents alongside their applications or services. Each OPA instance is responsible for processing authorization requests, fetching relevant policy data, and returning access control decisions to the calling application. OPA can be embedded directly into applications using its Go SDK or deployed as a sidecar service that handles authorization externally. Policy updates can be managed through centralized policy distribution mechanisms, where a control plane pushes new policies to all OPA instances dynamically.

OPA's strength lies in its ability to enforce policies across a wide range of systems, including API gateways (e.g., Kong, Envoy), Kubernetes admission controllers, and cloud security posture management tools. By defining policies centrally and enforcing them consistently across multiple services, organizations can maintain a unified access control model that adapts to evolving security requirements. OPA's decision logs provide transparency into policy evaluations, enabling security teams to audit authorization decisions, troubleshoot access issues, and refine policies based on real-world usage patterns.

Implementing dynamic authorization with OPA also enables advanced risk-based access control scenarios. Policies can incorporate real-time contextual data such as user location, device posture, and risk scores to make adaptive authorization decisions. For example, an API request from a trusted corporate network might be automatically permitted, whereas the same request from an unknown device in a high-risk location might require additional verification steps. This approach aligns with Zero Trust security principles by ensuring that access decisions are continuously evaluated based on real-time security context rather than static role assignments.

A hybrid approach that combines XACML and OPA can provide the best of both worlds for organizations with diverse authorization requirements. XACML's structured policy model is well-suited for enterprise-wide access control frameworks that require standardized policy enforcement across legacy and cloud applications. Meanwhile, OPA excels in enforcing policies at the infrastructure and microservices level, enabling granular authorization controls in dynamic environments. By integrating XACML-based policy decision points with OPA policy agents, organizations can achieve a comprehensive authorization model that scales across different application architectures.

Performance optimization in policy engines is a crucial consideration for large-scale IAM deployments. Both XACML and OPA can introduce latency in high-frequency authorization workflows if not properly optimized. To minimize performance overhead, policy engines should leverage caching mechanisms, distribute policy evaluations across multiple nodes, and reduce the complexity of policy rules. Precomputing authorization decisions for frequently accessed resources can further enhance efficiency, enabling rapid policy enforcement without excessive computation overhead.

The adoption of policy-driven IAM frameworks continues to grow as organizations prioritize security, compliance, and scalability in their access control strategies. Whether using XACML for standardized access control policies or OPA for dynamic microservices security, implementing a policy engine provides a flexible and scalable approach to enforcing fine-grained authorization decisions. As security landscapes evolve, organizations must continuously refine their policy models, monitor policy enforcement metrics, and adapt to emerging threats to ensure that access control remains effective across their digital ecosystems.

IAM Automation with Terraform, Ansible, and Kubernetes Operators

Automating Identity and Access Management (IAM) is essential for organizations looking to streamline identity provisioning, enforce security policies, and maintain compliance across cloud-native and hybrid environments. The manual management of IAM roles, permissions, service accounts, and access policies is not only time-consuming but also prone to human errors that can lead to security vulnerabilities. Infrastructure as Code (IaC) tools like Terraform, configuration management platforms such as Ansible, and Kubernetes Operators provide powerful automation capabilities for managing IAM resources efficiently. By leveraging these tools, security teams can implement scalable, repeatable, and policy-driven identity management solutions while reducing operational overhead.

Terraform, an open-source IaC tool, enables declarative management of IAM resources across multiple cloud providers and on-premises infrastructure. Using HashiCorp Configuration Language (HCL), security teams can define IAM roles, policies, groups, and service accounts as code, ensuring consistency and version control. Terraform's provider ecosystem includes modules for AWS IAM, Azure Active Directory, Google Cloud IAM, and third-party identity providers like Okta and Autho. By codifying IAM policies and role assignments in Terraform, organizations can enforce least privilege principles, audit access configurations, and automate the deployment of identity resources across multiple environments.

A key advantage of using Terraform for IAM automation is the ability to track IAM changes over time using version control systems like Git. Terraform configurations can be stored in repositories, allowing security teams to apply infrastructure-as-code best practices, such as pull request reviews, automated testing, and change tracking. The Terraform state file maintains a snapshot of deployed IAM resources, enabling controlled updates and preventing configuration drift. When IAM policies or permissions need to be modified, Terraform automatically determines the necessary changes and applies them in a predictable manner.

For organizations operating in multi-cloud environments, Terraform provides a unified approach to IAM management by abstracting provider-specific complexities. A single Terraform module can define IAM roles for AWS, Azure, and Google Cloud, ensuring consistent access policies across different platforms. Additionally, Terraform's support for dynamic input variables and conditional logic allows security teams to define reusable IAM configurations that adapt to different environments, such as development, staging, and production.

Ansible complements Terraform by providing procedural automation for IAM-related tasks that require real-time execution. While Terraform is primarily declarative and state-driven, Ansible excels at executing commands and configurations in a sequential manner. Ansible playbooks can be used to automate IAM operations such as user provisioning, password rotations, role-based access control (RBAC) enforcement, and identity synchronization. Unlike Terraform, which focuses on infrastructure provisioning, Ansible is well-suited for ongoing IAM policy enforcement and configuration management.

Ansible modules for IAM allow organizations to automate identity lifecycle management by integrating with directory services, cloud identity providers, and security tools. For example, Ansible can be used to automatically create new IAM users when an employee joins an organization, assign roles based on job function, and revoke access upon termination. Additionally, Ansible playbooks can enforce security policies by periodically auditing IAM configurations, detecting misconfigurations, and remediating policy violations.

In environments where IAM changes must be propagated across multiple systems, Ansible provides a powerful orchestration layer. An IAM automation workflow can be designed where Terraform provisions identity resources, and Ansible enforces security controls across cloud platforms, on-premises directories, and third-party applications. By combining Terraform's infrastructure-as-code capabilities with Ansible's task execution model, organizations can achieve comprehensive IAM automation that ensures consistency, compliance, and security.

Kubernetes Operators extend IAM automation into containerized environments by enabling policy-driven identity management for

Kubernetes workloads. Kubernetes does not natively provide fine-grained IAM capabilities, relying instead on external identity providers and role-based access control mechanisms. Kubernetes Operators bridge this gap by automating the deployment and lifecycle management of IAM policies, service accounts, and authentication mechanisms within Kubernetes clusters.

A Kubernetes Operator is a custom controller that automates the management of IAM-related resources within a Kubernetes cluster. Operators can be used to automatically provision service accounts, enforce network policies, and integrate Kubernetes workloads with cloud identity providers. For example, an IAM Operator for AWS can dynamically assign IAM roles to Kubernetes pods, ensuring that workloads have appropriate permissions without requiring static credentials. Similarly, an Azure AD-integrated Operator can automate user authentication and access control for Kubernetes applications running in Azure Kubernetes Service (AKS).

IAM Operators also facilitate the implementation of Just-In-Time (JIT) access controls within Kubernetes environments. By dynamically granting and revoking access based on real-time security policies, Operators help minimize the attack surface associated with long-lived credentials. Kubernetes-native IAM solutions such as Open Policy Agent (OPA) and Kyverno can be integrated with Operators to enforce fine-grained access control policies based on workload attributes, security contexts, and compliance requirements.

Automating IAM in Kubernetes environments requires careful consideration of secret management, identity federation, and API security. Kubernetes workloads often need to authenticate with cloud services, databases, and external APIs, requiring secure storage and distribution of credentials. IAM Operators can automate the management of Kubernetes Secrets, integrating with HashiCorp Vault, AWS Secrets Manager, and Azure Key Vault to securely inject secrets into containers. Additionally, Operators can enforce identity federation by integrating Kubernetes authentication with OpenID Connect (OIDC), enabling seamless single sign-on (SSO) across cloud and on-premises applications.

Scaling IAM automation across large enterprises and hybrid environments requires a combination of Terraform, Ansible, and Kubernetes Operators working together in a cohesive strategy. Terraform provides the foundation for defining and deploying IAM resources as code, ensuring consistent access policies across cloud providers. Ansible automates IAM tasks and enforces security policies in real-time, reducing administrative overhead. Kubernetes Operators extend IAM automation into containerized workloads, enabling dynamic identity management within cloud-native applications.

Security and compliance considerations must be integrated into IAM automation workflows to prevent misconfigurations and unauthorized access. Automated policy enforcement should include IAM auditing, anomaly detection, and compliance monitoring. Tools like AWS Config, Azure Policy, and Google Cloud Policy Intelligence can be integrated with Terraform and Ansible to continuously assess IAM configurations and enforce security best practices. Additionally, integrating IAM automation with Security Information and Event Management (SIEM) platforms allows organizations to monitor IAM-related security events and respond to potential threats proactively.

Automating IAM with Terraform, Ansible, and Kubernetes Operators not only improves security and compliance but also enhances operational efficiency. By eliminating manual IAM management tasks, organizations can reduce the risk of human error, accelerate identity provisioning, and enforce least privilege access controls consistently. As cloud environments become increasingly dynamic and distributed, IAM automation will continue to play a vital role in securing identities, mitigating risks, and ensuring that access control policies remain adaptive to evolving security requirements.

Real-Time Identity Event Processing using Kafka and Event-Driven Architectures

Modern Identity and Access Management (IAM) systems must be capable of processing identity events in real-time to detect security threats, enforce access policies dynamically, and ensure compliance with regulatory requirements. Traditional batch-based identity synchronization and access control mechanisms are no longer sufficient for cloud-native environments, where identities, roles, and permissions are constantly changing. Event-driven architectures, powered by Apache Kafka and other event streaming platforms, provide the scalability and flexibility needed to handle real-time identity event processing. By leveraging Kafka's distributed message streaming capabilities, IAM solutions can efficiently process authentication events, privilege escalations, login anomalies, and identity lifecycle changes as they occur.

Apache Kafka serves as a high-performance event streaming platform that enables IAM systems to ingest, process, and react to identity-related events in real-time. Unlike traditional request-response models that require synchronous processing, Kafka allows IAM components to operate asynchronously, decoupling event producers from consumers. This enables security teams to monitor and respond to identity changes without introducing latency into authentication and authorization workflows. Kafka's ability to handle massive volumes of streaming data ensures that IAM solutions can scale to accommodate millions of identity events per second across distributed environments.

Identity event processing in an event-driven IAM architecture begins with the generation of events at various sources, such as authentication servers, access control systems, cloud identity providers, and directory services. These events include login attempts, multi-factor authentication (MFA) challenges, user provisioning and deprovisioning actions, role changes, and policy enforcement decisions. Kafka acts as an event bus that captures these identity events and makes them available to downstream consumers, such as security analytics platforms, IAM policy engines, and automated remediation workflows.

One of the primary use cases for real-time identity event processing is anomaly detection in authentication activities. By streaming authentication logs into Kafka topics, IAM systems can continuously analyze login behavior, detect unusual access patterns, and trigger risk-based authentication mechanisms. For example, if a user logs in from an unfamiliar location or an untrusted device, a Kafka consumer can evaluate the risk level and enforce additional verification steps, such as requiring an MFA challenge or restricting access to certain resources. These real-time identity risk assessments enhance security by preventing credential abuse and account takeover attacks.

Privilege escalation monitoring is another critical application of event-driven IAM architectures. Changes to privileged accounts, role assignments, or access entitlements should be monitored in real-time to detect unauthorized or risky privilege modifications. By streaming IAM audit logs into Kafka, organizations can implement security policies that immediately flag suspicious privilege changes and trigger automated remediation actions, such as revoking excessive permissions, notifying security teams, or logging the event for forensic analysis.

User lifecycle management in IAM systems also benefits from real-time event processing. Traditionally, user provisioning and deprovisioning operations rely on scheduled synchronization jobs that update user accounts periodically. However, this batch-based approach introduces security risks, as access changes may not be reflected immediately across all systems. Event-driven architectures eliminate these delays by allowing identity updates to propagate instantly. When a new employee is onboarded, a Kafka event can trigger automated provisioning workflows that create user accounts, assign roles, and configure permissions in real time. Similarly, when an employee leaves an organization, Kafka can propagate deprovisioning events to revoke access instantly across all connected systems, reducing the risk of orphaned accounts.

IAM compliance auditing and reporting can also be enhanced using Kafka-based event processing. Security frameworks such as GDPR, HIPAA, and NIST 800-53 require organizations to maintain detailed audit logs of identity-related activities. Kafka provides a scalable solution for collecting, storing, and analyzing identity event logs, enabling security teams to generate compliance reports, detect policy violations, and respond to audit requests efficiently. By integrating Kafka with SIEM (Security Information and Event Management) platforms such as Splunk or ELK Stack, organizations can correlate identity events with other security signals, improving their ability to detect insider threats and external attacks.

Kafka's stream processing capabilities, enabled by Kafka Streams or Apache Flink, further enhance IAM automation by enabling real-time transformations and policy evaluations. Instead of simply forwarding raw events to downstream systems, stream processing allows IAM teams to enrich identity events with contextual information, apply policy-based filtering, and trigger automated workflows based on predefined conditions. For example, an identity event indicating an attempted login from a blacklisted IP address can be immediately processed by a Kafka stream, triggering an automatic account lockout or an alert to the security operations team.

In multi-cloud and hybrid IAM environments, Kafka facilitates identity event synchronization across disparate identity providers and cloud platforms. Organizations using AWS IAM, Azure AD, Google Cloud IAM, and on-premises Active Directory need a way to synchronize identity changes seamlessly. Kafka-based event hubs enable real-time replication of identity attributes, ensuring that user roles, group memberships, and access policies remain consistent across all environments. This is particularly valuable for enterprises undergoing digital transformation, where identities must be managed across multiple cloud service providers and legacy infrastructure.

Scalability and fault tolerance are essential considerations when implementing Kafka for IAM event processing. Kafka's distributed architecture allows IAM systems to handle high-throughput identity event streams without single points of failure. IAM platforms can deploy Kafka clusters with multiple brokers, ensuring redundancy and failover capabilities. Kafka's partitioning mechanism allows IAM workloads to be distributed across multiple nodes, enabling parallel processing of identity events for improved performance and scalability.

Security and access control for IAM event streams must also be enforced to prevent unauthorized access to sensitive identity data. Kafka supports role-based access control (RBAC) and authentication mechanisms such as TLS encryption, SASL authentication, and OAuth 2.0 integration. IAM systems must implement strict access policies to ensure that only authorized producers and consumers can publish and subscribe to identity event topics. Data encryption at rest and in transit protects identity-related information from interception or tampering.

Integration with microservices and API gateways further enhances the capabilities of Kafka-driven IAM architectures. IAM microservices can publish and consume identity events asynchronously, enabling scalable and loosely coupled authentication and authorization workflows. API gateways, such as Kong or Apigee, can integrate with Kafka to enforce real-time access control policies based on identity event streams. This allows IAM solutions to dynamically adjust API access permissions based on user behavior, device trust levels, or risk scores.

As IAM continues to evolve, event-driven architectures powered by Kafka provide a robust foundation for real-time identity event processing. By leveraging Kafka's capabilities, IAM systems can enhance security monitoring, enforce dynamic access control policies, improve user lifecycle management, and enable compliance automation. The ability to process identity events in real-time reduces security risks, accelerates IAM operations, and ensures that access control decisions align with the latest security intelligence. Organizations that adopt Kafka for IAM event streaming gain a powerful tool for managing identities at scale, securing authentication workflows, and responding to threats with speed and precision.

Programming Custom Authentication Flows using Java, Python, and Node.js

Developing custom authentication flows is an essential aspect of modern Identity and Access Management (IAM) systems, enabling organizations to enforce security policies, integrate with external identity providers, and support diverse authentication mechanisms. While many IAM platforms offer built-in authentication workflows, custom implementations are often required to accommodate unique business logic, regulatory requirements, and application-specific constraints. Programming authentication flows using Java, Python, and Node.js provides flexibility to implement multi-factor authentication (MFA), passwordless authentication, adaptive authentication, and federated identity solutions while maintaining control over security, performance, and user experience.

Java has long been a dominant language in enterprise IAM implementations, thanks to its strong ecosystem of security libraries and frameworks. Spring Security, a widely used authentication framework for Java applications, provides comprehensive support for authentication and authorization mechanisms, including OAuth 2.0, OpenID Connect (OIDC), and LDAP-based authentication. Implementing a custom authentication flow in Java typically involves extending AuthenticationProvider interfaces in Spring Security, allowing developers to integrate authentication logic such as verifying credentials against a custom database, calling external APIs, or implementing time-based one-time passwords (TOTP) for MFA.

A common use case for Java-based authentication is integrating with legacy identity stores that do not support modern authentication protocols. In such scenarios, developers can use Java Authentication and Authorization Service (JAAS) to interact with Kerberos, LDAP directories, or custom authentication backends. For applications requiring fine-grained access control, Java-based policy engines such as XACML (Extensible Access Control Markup Language) can be integrated with authentication flows to enforce dynamic authorization policies based on user attributes, session contexts, and risk factors.

Python is another powerful language for implementing authentication flows, particularly in web applications and cloud-native environments. Python's security libraries, such as Flask-Security and Django-Auth, provide out-of-the-box support for user authentication, session management, and token-based authentication. Implementing a custom authentication flow in Python often involves creating middleware components that process authentication requests, validate user credentials, and issue secure tokens.

One of the advantages of using Python for authentication is its flexibility in integrating with external identity providers. Python-based authentication flows can leverage OAuthLib to implement OAuth 2.0 authentication, allowing applications to delegate authentication to third-party providers such as Google, Microsoft Entra ID, or Okta. Additionally, Python's cryptographic libraries, such as PyJWT, enable secure token validation, ensuring that JSON Web Tokens (JWTs) are properly signed and contain valid claims before granting access to protected resources.

Python is also widely used in serverless authentication scenarios, where authentication logic is executed within AWS Lambda, Google Cloud Functions, or Azure Functions. In a serverless authentication flow, Python functions handle authentication requests, verify credentials against a database or external identity provider, and generate signed authentication tokens. This approach eliminates the need for dedicated authentication servers, reducing infrastructure complexity while maintaining security and scalability.

Node.js has become a preferred choice for implementing authentication in modern web and API-based applications due to its asynchronous nature and strong support for authentication frameworks. Express.js, a popular web framework for Node.js, provides middleware such as passport.js to implement authentication flows using strategies such as local authentication, OAuth 2.0, and SAML. Developing custom authentication flows in Node.js typically involves defining middleware functions that intercept authentication requests, validate credentials, and manage user sessions.

One of the key strengths of Node.js for authentication is its ability to handle real-time authentication scenarios. WebSocket-based authentication, commonly used in chat applications and live data streaming platforms, can be implemented using JWTs and authentication middleware in Node.js. By maintaining secure WebSocket connections and enforcing token-based authentication, Node.js applications can ensure that only authorized users can establish real-time communication channels.

Another powerful feature of Node.js authentication flows is its integration with biometric authentication mechanisms. Modern authentication solutions, such as WebAuthn, allow users to authenticate using fingerprint readers, facial recognition, or hardware security keys. Node.js libraries such as fido2-lib enable developers to implement WebAuthn authentication flows, allowing applications to offer passwordless authentication with strong cryptographic security.

Custom authentication flows often require multi-factor authentication (MFA) to enhance security. Implementing MFA in Java, Python, or Node.js typically involves generating and verifying TOTP-based codes, sending push notifications, or integrating with SMS-based authentication providers. For example, in a Node.js authentication flow, an application can generate a TOTP code using the otplib library and send it to the user's registered device for verification before completing the authentication process. Similarly, a Python-based authentication service can integrate with Twilio or AWS SNS to send one-time passwords via SMS, ensuring that authentication is secured with an additional verification step.

Adaptive authentication is another critical feature in custom authentication flows, allowing IAM systems to adjust authentication requirements based on user risk profiles. Implementing adaptive authentication in Java, Python, or Node.js involves analyzing contextual factors such as geolocation, device reputation, and login behavior. If a login attempt is detected from an unusual location or a high-risk device, the authentication flow can trigger additional verification steps, such as requiring a second authentication factor or prompting for biometric authentication.

Federated authentication, which enables users to authenticate across multiple applications using a single identity provider, is commonly implemented in custom authentication flows. Java, Python, and Node.js applications can integrate with identity federation protocols such as SAML and OIDC to support Single Sign-On (SSO) across multiple services. In a Java-based authentication flow, developers can use spring-security-saml2-service-provider to implement SAML-based authentication with enterprise identity providers. In Python, python-saml provides similar capabilities, allowing applications to process SAML authentication assertions and establish trust relationships with external IdPs.

Security is a fundamental aspect of programming custom authentication flows, requiring careful implementation of encryption, token validation, and session management. Java-based authentication flows should enforce strong encryption using JCA (Java Cryptography Architecture) to protect credentials and authentication tokens. Python applications should use Argon2 or bcrypt for secure password hashing, preventing credential leaks from password databases. Node.js authentication flows should implement HTTPS enforcement, token expiration policies, and request signing mechanisms to prevent authentication bypass attacks.

Implementing robust logging and monitoring in authentication flows helps detect suspicious authentication attempts, unauthorized access, and credential stuffing attacks. Logging authentication events in centralized security monitoring systems, such as Splunk or ELK Stack, enables security teams to analyze authentication patterns, detect anomalies, and respond to security threats in real-time. Additionally, integrating authentication logs with Security Information and Event Management (SIEM) platforms allows automated threat detection and response based on authentication event data.

As authentication technologies evolve, custom authentication flows must adapt to support emerging authentication standards and security best practices. Java, Python, and Node.js provide the flexibility and extensibility needed to implement secure, scalable, and adaptive authentication mechanisms that align with modern IAM requirements. By leveraging these languages, organizations can develop authentication solutions that enhance security, improve user experience, and integrate seamlessly with cloud-based and enterprise IAM systems.

Building Custom Multi-Factor Authentication (MFA) Solutions with FIDO2/WebAuthn

Multi-Factor Authentication (MFA) is a critical component of modern Identity and Access Management (IAM), ensuring that users authenticate using multiple independent factors to enhance security beyond traditional password-based authentication. As cyber threats evolve, attackers increasingly exploit weak passwords, credential stuffing, and phishing attacks to compromise user accounts. To mitigate these risks, organizations are implementing MFA solutions based on the Fast Identity Online (FIDO2) standard and the Web Authentication (WebAuthn) API, which enable passwordless authentication and strong cryptographic security. Building a custom MFA solution using FIDO2/WebAuthn allows organizations to enforce high-assurance authentication while improving user experience and reducing reliance on insecure credentials.

FIDO2 is an open authentication standard developed by the FIDO Alliance, designed to provide phishing-resistant authentication using cryptographic key pairs stored on secure hardware devices. WebAuthn, a core component of FIDO2, is a web-based API that enables browsers and applications to interact with authentication devices such as security keys, biometric sensors, and trusted platform modules (TPMs). Unlike traditional MFA methods, which rely on SMS-based one-time passwords (OTPs) or mobile authentication apps, FIDO2/WebAuthn provides a more secure and seamless authentication experience by leveraging public key cryptography.

A custom MFA solution built with FIDO2/WebAuthn consists of several components: a user enrollment process, an authentication flow, a secure backend for managing credentials, and an integration layer for web and mobile applications. The first step in implementing WebAuthn-based MFA is user registration, where the user enrolls a trusted authentication device, such as a FIDO2 security key, a fingerprint scanner, or a facial recognition sensor. During this process, the authentication device generates a public-private key pair, securely storing the private key on the device while sending the public key to the authentication server. The server associates the public key with the user's identity and stores it in a secure database.

To facilitate WebAuthn registration, applications must integrate with the WebAuthn API, which is supported by modern browsers such as Chrome, Firefox, Edge, and Safari. The registration process begins when the user initiates device enrollment through the application's authentication portal. The server generates a WebAuthn challenge and sends it to the user's device, prompting the authentication hardware to create a new key pair. Once the key pair is generated, the public key and related metadata are sent to the server, completing the registration process. The metadata includes information about the device, such as attestation data that verifies its authenticity and security properties.

Authentication with WebAuthn follows a similar flow, except that instead of generating a new key pair, the authentication device signs a challenge using the previously registered private key. When a user attempts to log in, the authentication server issues a challenge, which the WebAuthn client (browser or mobile app) sends to the authentication device. The device signs the challenge using the stored private key and returns the signed response to the server, which verifies the signature using the registered public key. If the verification is successful, the user is granted access.

One of the key advantages of WebAuthn-based MFA is its resistance to phishing attacks. Unlike traditional MFA methods, which rely on manually entered codes or push notifications, WebAuthn authentication is bound to the origin of the requesting application. This prevents attackers from stealing authentication credentials through fake login pages or man-in-the-middle attacks. Additionally, WebAuthn credentials are device-bound, meaning they cannot be easily duplicated or transferred to another device without user consent.

For organizations implementing custom MFA solutions, integrating WebAuthn with existing IAM platforms requires careful consideration of security policies, device management, and fallback authentication mechanisms. While WebAuthn provides a highly secure authentication method, organizations must support fallback authentication methods for users who lose access to their authentication devices. Backup authentication options may include time-based OTPs (TOTP), recovery codes, or hardware token backups. However, fallback mechanisms should be designed with strict security policies to prevent social engineering attacks or account takeovers.

Custom WebAuthn implementations also require secure backend storage for registered public keys and user authentication metadata. Public keys should be stored in an encrypted database with strict access controls, ensuring that only authorized services can access credential data. Additionally, organizations should implement audit logging for WebAuthn registration and authentication events, allowing security teams to monitor for anomalies and unauthorized access attempts.

WebAuthn supports both platform authenticators (built into user devices, such as Windows Hello or Apple Face ID) and roaming authenticators (external security keys, such as YubiKeys or Titan Security Keys). A robust MFA solution should allow users to register multiple authentication devices, providing flexibility for different authentication scenarios. For example, a user may register both a fingerprint sensor on their laptop for daily authentication and a hardware security key for use when traveling or accessing highly sensitive systems.

For enterprises adopting WebAuthn-based MFA, integrating authentication policies with IAM governance frameworks is essential. Organizations can define access policies based on risk factors, requiring WebAuthn authentication for high-risk transactions or administrative actions. Adaptive authentication mechanisms can enforce step-up authentication based on user behavior, device reputation, or geographic location. By combining WebAuthn with risk-based authentication, organizations can enhance security without introducing unnecessary friction for users.

Mobile applications can leverage WebAuthn for secure authentication by integrating with platform-specific authentication APIs, such as Android's BiometricPrompt API and Apple's Face ID/Touch ID authentication framework. By using WebAuthn-compatible libraries, mobile applications can provide a seamless authentication experience while maintaining strong security protections. Additionally, WebAuthn can be combined with Single Sign-On (SSO) solutions to enable federated authentication across multiple applications without requiring repeated authentication steps.

One of the challenges in implementing WebAuthn-based MFA is ensuring compatibility across different browsers, devices, and operating systems. While WebAuthn is widely supported in modern browsers, some legacy applications or enterprise environments may require additional compatibility measures. Organizations should conduct extensive testing to ensure that WebAuthn authentication works across different user devices and implement fallback authentication paths for unsupported environments.

Performance optimization is another consideration for custom WebAuthn-based MFA solutions. Authentication latency should be minimized to ensure a smooth user experience, particularly for large-scale IAM deployments with high authentication traffic. Caching mechanisms, load balancing, and efficient cryptographic operations help improve WebAuthn authentication performance while maintaining security.

FIDO2/WebAuthn represents a significant advancement in authentication security, providing a scalable and phishing-resistant alternative to traditional MFA methods. By developing custom WebAuthn-based MFA solutions, organizations can enhance security while reducing user friction and eliminating the risks associated with password-based authentication. A well-implemented WebAuthn solution integrates seamlessly with existing IAM platforms, enforces strong authentication policies, and provides users with a secure, frictionless authentication experience.

Implementing Certificate-Based Authentication (CBA) and Smart Cards in IAM

Certificate-Based Authentication (CBA) and smart card authentication provide highly secure identity verification methods in Identity and Access Management (IAM) systems. These methods leverage cryptographic certificates and hardware-based authentication to ensure strong, phishing-resistant authentication that is significantly more secure than traditional password-based authentication. Organizations that require high levels of security, such as government agencies, financial institutions, and enterprises handling sensitive data, implement CBA and smart cards to enforce strict access control policies, eliminate password vulnerabilities, and ensure compliance with security regulations.

CBA is based on the use of X.509 digital certificates, which are issued by a trusted Certificate Authority (CA) and securely stored on client devices, smart cards, or hardware security modules (HSMs). These certificates contain cryptographic key pairs—one private key securely stored on the authentication device and a corresponding public key that is used for verification. When a user attempts to authenticate, their device presents the public key certificate, and the system verifies the certificate's authenticity before granting access. This authentication method ensures that credentials cannot be easily stolen or reused, making it resistant to credential-based attacks such as phishing, brute force, and password spraying.

One of the core components of CBA is the Public Key Infrastructure (PKI), which establishes a hierarchy of trust through Root CAs, Intermediate CAs, and client certificates. The PKI ensures that certificates used for authentication are issued and validated through a chain of trust. When a user presents a certificate for authentication, the IAM system checks the certificate's validity against the CA, ensuring that it has not expired, been revoked, or issued by an untrusted source. Organizations implement Online Certificate Status Protocol (OCSP) and Certificate Revocation Lists (CRLs) to verify certificate status in real-time and revoke compromised or expired certificates.

Smart cards extend the capabilities of CBA by providing a portable, tamper-resistant authentication device that securely stores user credentials, private keys, and digital certificates. These cards are typically used in conjunction with a smart card reader or Near Field Communication (NFC)-enabled device to facilitate secure authentication. Smart card authentication is commonly used in enterprise environments, government agencies, and military organizations to enforce strong identity verification and access control measures. By requiring physical possession of the smart card in addition to a PIN or biometric verification, organizations implement two-factor authentication (2FA) that is more resistant to remote attacks.

Integrating smart cards and CBA into IAM systems requires careful planning to ensure seamless authentication experiences while maintaining strong security policies. Many enterprise IAM solutions, including Microsoft Active Directory Certificate Services (ADCS), Red Hat Identity Management, and OpenSSL-based PKI implementations, support smart card authentication and certificate validation. Organizations deploying smart card-based authentication must establish a robust enrollment process, ensuring that certificates are securely issued, distributed, and renewed without exposing private keys to unauthorized entities.

Smart card authentication is commonly used for workstation login, remote access, and privileged access management. In enterprise environments, organizations enforce smart card authentication as a mandatory login method for employees accessing corporate systems.

When users insert their smart card into a reader, the system verifies the digital certificate, checks the validity of the issuing CA, and prompts the user for a PIN or biometric verification. This prevents unauthorized access, as attackers cannot gain entry without possessing the physical smart card and knowing the associated authentication factors.

For remote access scenarios, CBA and smart cards integrate with Virtual Private Networks (VPNs), remote desktop protocols (RDP), and cloud-based authentication gateways. Secure VPN authentication using smart cards ensures that only trusted users with valid certificates can establish remote connections to enterprise networks. By enforcing client certificate validation, organizations prevent unauthorized devices from accessing sensitive systems. Cloud IAM providers such as Microsoft Entra ID, Okta, and Ping Identity offer support for CBA, allowing organizations to implement certificate-based Single Sign-On (SSO) for web applications, cloud services, and federated identity providers.

One of the key challenges in deploying smart card authentication is managing certificate lifecycle events, including issuance, renewal, and revocation. IAM systems must integrate with PKI solutions to automate certificate provisioning and enforce expiration policies. When a certificate reaches its expiration date or is revoked due to compromise, the IAM system should immediately prevent authentication using that certificate. Implementing automated certificate management solutions such as HashiCorp Vault, Keycloak, or Venafi helps streamline certificate issuance and renewal processes while reducing administrative overhead.

Security policies for CBA and smart cards should enforce strong cryptographic standards, ensuring that certificates use modern, secure algorithms such as RSA-4096, ECC-P256, or post-quantum cryptographic schemes. Legacy cryptographic algorithms such as SHA-1 and RSA-1024 are no longer considered secure and should be deprecated in favor of stronger encryption methods. Organizations must also enforce secure key storage, ensuring that private keys are never exported or stored in insecure locations. Hardware-backed security modules, including Trusted Platform Modules (TPMs) and

FIPS-compliant smart cards, provide additional layers of protection against key extraction and credential compromise.

For organizations implementing Zero Trust architectures, CBA and smart cards serve as a fundamental component of identity verification and continuous authentication. Instead of relying solely on initial authentication events, Zero Trust security models enforce continuous verification by requiring smart card-based re-authentication for high-risk transactions, privileged access requests, or network segmentation policies. By combining CBA with behavioral analytics and risk-based authentication, organizations strengthen their security posture against evolving cyber threats.

Compliance with security standards and regulatory frameworks is another critical factor in implementing CBA and smart cards. Many industries, including finance, healthcare, and defense, mandate strong authentication measures to protect sensitive data and comply with regulations such as NIST 800-63, GDPR, PCI-DSS, and HIPAA. CBA and smart cards align with these security standards by providing non-repudiation, strong identity verification, and secure authentication that meets regulatory requirements. Organizations undergoing security audits can demonstrate compliance by implementing centralized logging, certificate audit trails, and IAM governance policies that enforce CBA authentication for high-privilege accounts.

The adoption of smart cards and CBA in cloud-native environments requires integration with modern authentication protocols such as OAuth 2.0, SAML, and OpenID Connect. Cloud identity providers support certificate-based authentication by issuing short-lived tokens that allow users to authenticate to cloud services without exposing private keys. Organizations leveraging cloud IAM solutions must implement secure APIs and authentication gateways that validate certificates and enforce access control policies dynamically.

As cybersecurity threats become more sophisticated, organizations must adopt strong authentication measures that prevent unauthorized access and credential theft. Certificate-Based Authentication and smart card authentication provide a highly secure, scalable solution for IAM systems, eliminating password-based vulnerabilities and enforcing strong identity assurance across enterprise networks, cloud environments, and privileged access scenarios. By integrating CBA with modern IAM platforms, automating certificate lifecycle management, and enforcing security best practices, organizations can achieve a robust authentication framework that meets the highest security standards.

Cryptographic Key Management for IAM: HSMs, PKI, and Hardware-Based Security

Cryptographic key management is a fundamental component of Identity and Access Management (IAM), ensuring that authentication, authorization, and encryption mechanisms are secure and resistant to attacks. Managing cryptographic keys involves generating, storing, distributing, rotating, and revoking keys while maintaining strict security controls to prevent unauthorized access and misuse. In modern IAM implementations, Hardware Security Modules (HSMs), Public Key Infrastructure (PKI), and hardware-based security solutions provide the necessary mechanisms to protect sensitive cryptographic operations and secure user identities. Proper key management is essential for ensuring the integrity of authentication systems, protecting credentials, securing digital certificates, and enforcing compliance with industry standards and regulations.

Public Key Infrastructure (PKI) is a foundational technology for cryptographic key management in IAM, enabling secure digital identity verification through asymmetric cryptography. PKI relies on a hierarchy of trusted entities, including Certificate Authorities (CAs), Registration Authorities (RAs), and certificate repositories, to issue and manage digital certificates. Each certificate contains a public key that is linked to an entity's identity, allowing authentication and encryption operations to be securely performed. PKI plays a crucial role in securing IAM systems by enabling Certificate-Based Authentication (CBA), digital signatures, and encrypted communication channels.

Key generation in PKI is a critical process that must be handled securely to prevent key compromise. Cryptographic keys must be generated using high-entropy sources and stored in secure environments that prevent unauthorized access. Hardware Security Modules (HSMs) are dedicated cryptographic devices designed to securely generate, store, and manage cryptographic keys while protecting them from extraction or tampering. Unlike software-based key storage solutions, which are vulnerable to malware and insider threats, HSMs provide physical and logical security measures that prevent key exfiltration. Organizations that require high levels of security, such as financial institutions and government agencies, rely on HSMs to protect root CA private keys, encryption keys, and authentication tokens.

HSMs are commonly used in IAM architectures to secure authentication tokens, protect secrets, and enforce strong cryptographic policies. Many enterprise IAM solutions, including Microsoft Entra ID, AWS IAM, and Google Cloud IAM, support HSM-backed key management to ensure secure authentication and data encryption. HSMs integrate with IAM systems to enable secure signing of digital certificates, hardware-backed key attestation, and tamper-resistant key storage. When an IAM system needs to issue a cryptographic token, sign an authentication request, or encrypt sensitive identity attributes, it offloads these operations to the HSM to ensure that private keys are never exposed in memory or software.

In cloud-based IAM environments, Cloud HSMs provide the same level of security as on-premises HSMs while offering scalability and integration with cloud identity providers. Cloud-based HSM solutions, such as AWS CloudHSM, Azure Key Vault Managed HSM, and Google Cloud HSM, enable organizations to store and manage cryptographic keys securely without maintaining on-premises hardware. These services offer high-availability key storage, automatic key rotation, and integration with IAM policies to enforce access control over cryptographic operations.

Key rotation and lifecycle management are essential aspects of cryptographic key security in IAM. Long-lived cryptographic keys increase the risk of compromise, making regular key rotation a critical security measure. IAM systems must implement automated key rotation policies that periodically generate new key pairs, update certificates, and deprecate old keys. HSMs and PKI solutions provide mechanisms for automated key renewal and revocation, ensuring that outdated or compromised keys cannot be used for authentication or encryption. Key revocation lists (CRLs) and Online Certificate Status

Protocol (OCSP) responders allow IAM systems to verify the validity of digital certificates in real time and prevent the use of revoked credentials.

Hardware-based security extends beyond HSMs and PKI to include Trusted Platform Modules (TPMs) and Secure Elements (SEs), which provide cryptographic key protection at the device level. TPMs are embedded security chips that enable hardware-based authentication, disk encryption, and secure key storage for endpoint devices. In IAM implementations, TPMs are used to protect authentication tokens, store biometric credentials, and enforce device attestation policies. Secure Elements, found in smart cards and hardware security keys, provide similar functionality for identity authentication, ensuring that private keys never leave the secure hardware environment.

For IAM systems that implement passwordless authentication, cryptographic key management plays a crucial role in securing authentication credentials. FIDO2/WebAuthn authentication relies on asymmetric cryptography, where private keys are stored in HSMs, TPMs, or Secure Elements while public keys are registered with the IAM system. By eliminating password-based authentication and leveraging hardware-backed key storage, organizations can prevent credential theft, phishing attacks, and brute-force login attempts.

API security in IAM also depends on cryptographic key management, ensuring that OAuth 2.0 tokens, JSON Web Tokens (JWTs), and API keys are securely generated, signed, and validated. IAM systems must implement secure key management practices for signing authentication tokens, verifying token integrity, and enforcing expiration policies. HSM-backed key signing prevents unauthorized token generation and ensures that signed tokens cannot be tampered with. Additionally, secure key exchange mechanisms, such as Diffie-Hellman key agreement and Elliptic Curve Cryptography (ECC), enable IAM APIs to establish encrypted communication channels with clients and identity providers.

Compliance with security standards and regulatory frameworks requires strict cryptographic key management policies in IAM systems. Regulations such as PCI-DSS, GDPR, HIPAA, and NIST 800-57 mandate strong encryption and key protection measures to secure authentication credentials and sensitive identity data. IAM solutions must implement encryption at rest and in transit, enforce key access controls, and maintain audit logs of cryptographic operations to ensure compliance. Organizations undergoing security audits must demonstrate that cryptographic keys are securely generated, stored, and rotated according to industry best practices.

IAM systems that support federated authentication and Single Sign-On (SSO) require strong cryptographic key management to establish secure trust relationships between identity providers (IdPs) and service providers (SPs). SAML assertions, OAuth access tokens, and OIDC ID tokens must be signed using secure private keys to prevent token forgery and replay attacks. Federated IAM architectures must implement distributed key management solutions that enable secure cross-domain authentication while ensuring that keys remain protected from unauthorized access.

Disaster recovery and business continuity planning for IAM cryptographic keys are critical to preventing authentication failures and ensuring system availability. Organizations must implement secure key backup and recovery procedures to protect against data loss, hardware failures, and insider threats. HSMs and PKI solutions provide key escrow mechanisms that enable secure key recovery in the event of system failure. IAM teams must define strict policies for key restoration, ensuring that only authorized personnel can access backup keys and that recovery operations are securely logged.

Advancements in cryptographic key management continue to evolve as organizations adopt post-quantum cryptography and zero-trust security models. Quantum-resistant encryption algorithms are being developed to future-proof IAM systems against potential quantum computing threats. Additionally, zero-trust IAM architectures require continuous verification of authentication credentials, enforcing strict cryptographic policies for device identity, session tokens, and privileged access keys. By implementing strong cryptographic key management practices, leveraging HSMs, and integrating PKI-based authentication, organizations can build resilient IAM systems that protect user identities, secure authentication processes, and prevent unauthorized access.

Building Serverless IAM Solutions using AWS Lambda, Azure Functions, and Google Cloud Functions

Identity and Access Management (IAM) is a crucial component of modern cloud security, enabling organizations to enforce authentication, authorization, and identity lifecycle management. Traditional IAM implementations rely on persistent servers and infrastructure to handle identity verification, token issuance, and policy enforcement. However, as cloud environments evolve, serverless computing has emerged as an efficient, scalable, and cost-effective approach to managing IAM operations. By leveraging serverless platforms such as AWS Lambda, Azure Functions, and Google Cloud Functions, organizations can build highly available IAM solutions that dynamically scale with demand while minimizing infrastructure overhead.

Serverless IAM solutions operate on the principle of event-driven computing, where authentication and authorization workflows are triggered in response to identity-related events. Unlike traditional IAM systems that require dedicated servers for processing authentication requests, serverless IAM functions execute only when needed, reducing costs and eliminating the need for long-running authentication services. These functions can integrate with cloud identity providers, database services, and API gateways to perform critical IAM tasks such as user authentication, token validation, policy enforcement, and identity synchronization.

AWS Lambda provides a powerful platform for building serverless IAM solutions by integrating with AWS Identity and Access Management (IAM), Amazon Cognito, and AWS Security Token Service (STS). Organizations can use AWS Lambda to implement custom authentication flows, enforce access policies, and automate identity provisioning. For example, when a user attempts to log in via Amazon Cognito, a Lambda function can be triggered to validate credentials, perform multi-factor authentication (MFA), and generate access tokens. Lambda functions can also enforce dynamic authorization policies by evaluating user attributes, roles, and contextual factors before granting access to AWS resources.

In addition to authentication and authorization, AWS Lambda can be used to automate identity lifecycle management. When a new user account is created in an enterprise directory, a Lambda function can synchronize identity attributes with AWS IAM roles, ensuring that the user has appropriate permissions across AWS services. Similarly, when an employee leaves the organization, Lambda functions can be triggered to revoke access, remove IAM policies, and disable API keys. By automating these processes, organizations can reduce security risks associated with orphaned accounts and privilege creep.

Azure Functions offers a similar approach to building serverless IAM solutions within the Microsoft cloud ecosystem. Azure Functions can integrate with Microsoft Entra ID (formerly Azure Active Directory) to enable seamless authentication, role-based access control (RBAC), and token validation. Serverless IAM workflows in Azure often involve triggering functions in response to Microsoft Entra ID events, such as user logins, password changes, or group membership updates. For example, an Azure Function can be used to verify user authentication tokens, enforce conditional access policies, and log authentication events for security auditing.

One of the key advantages of using Azure Functions for IAM is the ability to integrate with Microsoft Graph API, which provides access to identity and directory data. Serverless functions can query user attributes, retrieve group memberships, and apply access policies in real-time. Organizations can use this capability to build adaptive authentication mechanisms that adjust access levels based on user behavior, device trust levels, and security risk assessments. Azure Functions can also facilitate Just-In-Time (JIT) access provisioning, where temporary permissions are granted to users based on specific tasks and automatically revoked after a defined period.

Google Cloud Functions provides a serverless environment for implementing IAM solutions within Google Cloud Platform (GCP). By integrating with Google Cloud IAM, Cloud Identity, and Firebase Authentication, organizations can build scalable authentication and authorization services without managing dedicated infrastructure.

Cloud Functions can be triggered by authentication events in Firebase Authentication, allowing developers to customize user authentication flows, enforce additional security checks, and log access attempts for compliance monitoring.

A common use case for Google Cloud Functions in IAM is enforcing fine-grained access control to cloud resources. When a user or service account attempts to access a Google Cloud resource, a Cloud Function can intercept the request, evaluate access policies, and approve or deny access based on predefined security rules. This approach allows organizations to implement attribute-based access control (ABAC) dynamically, ensuring that permissions are granted based on user attributes, project context, and real-time security signals.

Serverless IAM solutions can also enhance API security by integrating with API gateways and identity providers. AWS API Gateway, Azure API Management, and Google Cloud Endpoints allow organizations to enforce authentication and authorization at the API level using serverless functions. For instance, a Lambda function can validate OAuth 2.0 access tokens before processing API requests, ensuring that only authorized users and applications can access protected resources. Similarly, Azure Functions and Cloud Functions can be used to validate JSON Web Tokens (JWTs), perform role-based access checks, and log API authentication events for auditing purposes.

Multi-factor authentication (MFA) can be implemented using serverless IAM functions to improve security posture. AWS Lambda can integrate with Amazon Cognito to enforce MFA requirements, such as sending one-time passwords (OTPs) via SMS or email. Azure Functions can interact with Microsoft Authenticator to prompt users for biometric authentication before granting access to sensitive data. Google Cloud Functions can trigger Firebase Authentication MFA flows, requiring users to verify their identity using trusted devices. By leveraging serverless functions for MFA, organizations can enforce strong authentication measures without maintaining dedicated authentication servers.

Security and compliance are critical considerations when implementing serverless IAM solutions. Serverless functions should follow the principle of least privilege, ensuring that functions only have the necessary permissions to perform specific IAM tasks. AWS Lambda execution roles, Azure Managed Identities, and Google Cloud IAM roles should be carefully scoped to prevent unauthorized access to identity data and authentication services. Additionally, logging and monitoring should be integrated into serverless IAM functions to detect and respond to authentication anomalies. AWS CloudTrail, Azure Monitor, and Google Cloud Logging can be used to track IAM-related events, providing visibility into authentication attempts, access policy changes, and privilege escalations.

Performance optimization is another important factor in serverless IAM implementations. Since serverless functions operate on-demand, cold start latency can impact authentication workflows. To mitigate this, organizations can use provisioned concurrency in AWS Lambda, Azure Premium Functions, or Google Cloud Functions with pre-warmed instances to ensure low-latency execution of authentication requests. Additionally, caching strategies can be applied to store frequently accessed IAM policies, reducing the need for repeated authorization lookups.

By leveraging AWS Lambda, Azure Functions, and Google Cloud Functions, organizations can build highly scalable, cost-effective IAM solutions that adapt to modern security requirements. Serverless IAM implementations eliminate the need for dedicated authentication servers, reduce infrastructure complexity, and enable real-time identity processing through event-driven architectures. Whether securing cloud applications, enforcing fine-grained access controls, or automating identity lifecycle management, serverless IAM functions provide a flexible and resilient approach to managing identities in dynamic cloud environments.

Developing Custom IAM Dashboards and Self-Service Portals using React and GraphQL

Identity and Access Management (IAM) solutions require intuitive and user-friendly interfaces to streamline identity administration, access requests, and user self-service functionalities. Traditional IAM platforms often rely on complex, cumbersome interfaces that require manual intervention from IT administrators, leading to inefficiencies and delays in identity operations. Developing custom IAM dashboards and self-service portals using modern web technologies such as React and GraphQL enables organizations to provide a seamless user experience while maintaining strong security controls. By leveraging React's component-based architecture and GraphQL's efficient data-fetching capabilities, IAM dashboards can be built with real-time updates, dynamic user interactions, and scalable identity management functionalities.

React is a powerful JavaScript library designed for building interactive web applications with reusable components. Its virtual DOM (Document Object Model) ensures efficient rendering, making it ideal for developing IAM dashboards that require real-time data updates. A well-designed IAM dashboard in React provides administrators and users with an intuitive interface to manage identities, roles, permissions, and access policies. The flexibility of React allows developers to build modular IAM components such as user management tables, access request workflows, multi-factor authentication (MFA) configuration panels, and audit logs visualization.

GraphQL serves as a robust API layer that simplifies data retrieval and enhances performance in IAM applications. Unlike REST APIs, which require multiple round trips to fetch related data, GraphQL allows clients to query exactly what they need in a single request. This efficiency is crucial for IAM dashboards that display complex identity data, such as nested user attributes, role hierarchies, and access control policies. By integrating GraphQL with an IAM backend, the frontend React application can retrieve identity-related information dynamically, reducing API response times and improving application performance.

The architecture of a custom IAM dashboard using React and GraphQL consists of several key components, including authentication mechanisms, role-based access control (RBAC), self-service user functionalities, and administrative tools for managing access policies. Authentication is the foundation of IAM portals, ensuring that only authorized users can access identity management features. React applications can integrate with authentication providers using OAuth 2.0, OpenID Connect (OIDC), or JSON Web Tokens (JWTs) to establish secure user sessions. Upon login, the dashboard retrieves user details, permissions, and available IAM operations from the GraphQL API, dynamically rendering UI elements based on the user's access level.

Role-based access control (RBAC) is a critical aspect of IAM dashboards, enabling organizations to enforce granular permissions for different user roles. React applications can leverage GraphQL queries to fetch user roles and dynamically display authorized actions within the interface. For example, an administrator logging into the IAM dashboard may have access to identity governance workflows, audit logs, and user provisioning tools, while a regular employee may only have access to personal profile settings and access request forms. GraphQL mutations allow users to update their roles, request additional permissions, or escalate access approvals without requiring manual intervention from IT administrators.

Self-service IAM portals empower users to manage their own identities, reducing administrative overhead while improving security compliance. React-based self-service portals provide users with intuitive workflows for password resets, MFA enrollment, access request submissions, and device management. A well-designed self-service portal eliminates the need for IT helpdesk intervention by allowing users to securely update personal details, manage security credentials, and track access requests in real-time. GraphQL subscriptions enable real-time updates, ensuring that changes in access policies, authentication status, or user attributes are reflected immediately within the portal interface.

Multi-factor authentication (MFA) configuration is another essential feature of custom IAM dashboards. React applications can integrate with authentication providers to offer users the ability to enable or disable MFA settings, register authentication devices, and generate backup recovery codes. GraphQL queries retrieve the user's current authentication status, while mutations allow them to enroll new authentication factors such as biometric authentication, hardware security keys, or one-time password (OTP) generators. The real-time nature of GraphQL subscriptions ensures that MFA changes are synchronized across all devices, preventing security gaps in authentication workflows.

Audit logs and identity monitoring tools provide administrators with visibility into IAM events, ensuring compliance with security policies and regulatory requirements. React-based dashboards can display detailed audit logs, capturing authentication attempts, access changes, role modifications, and policy violations. GraphQL enables efficient filtering of audit data, allowing administrators to drill down into specific events, track anomalies, and generate compliance reports. Integrating IAM dashboards with Security Information and Event Management (SIEM) systems enhances threat detection, enabling organizations to respond proactively to identity-related security incidents.

Custom IAM dashboards also facilitate access request workflows, enabling users to request additional privileges based on business needs. React-based interfaces provide an intuitive experience for users to search for available roles, submit access requests, and track approval statuses. GraphQL enables seamless data fetching, allowing users to view pending approvals, justification requirements, and decision timelines. Workflow automation ensures that access requests are routed through appropriate approval channels, reducing manual review time and enforcing compliance with least privilege principles.

Scalability and performance optimization are critical when developing IAM dashboards for large enterprises. React's component-based structure allows for efficient state management using tools like Redux or React Context, ensuring that identity data updates do not impact application performance. GraphQL caching mechanisms and pagination strategies help optimize API responses, reducing the load on IAM backends and improving query performance. Deploying IAM dashboards in cloud environments with Content Delivery Networks (CDNs) and server-side rendering (SSR) further enhances performance, ensuring low-latency access for global users.

Security best practices must be enforced in custom IAM dashboards to protect sensitive identity data from unauthorized access. React applications should implement strict access controls, encrypt user sessions, and sanitize input fields to prevent cross-site scripting (XSS) and SQL injection attacks. GraphQL APIs should enforce role-based authorization, ensuring that queries and mutations are executed only by authorized users. Implementing GraphQL rate limiting and query depth restrictions prevents abuse and mitigates the risk of GraphQL injection attacks.

Deployment and integration considerations play a crucial role in ensuring the success of custom IAM dashboards. React-based IAM applications can be deployed as standalone portals or integrated within existing enterprise applications. GraphQL backends can be hosted using cloud services such as AWS AppSync, Hasura, or Apollo Server, ensuring seamless scalability and security. IAM dashboards should integrate with existing authentication providers, directory services, and identity governance platforms to provide a unified access management experience across the organization.

By leveraging React and GraphQL, organizations can build highly functional, user-friendly IAM dashboards and self-service portals that improve identity management efficiency, enhance security compliance, and empower users with self-service capabilities. The combination of React's dynamic UI components and GraphQL's efficient data querying enables the creation of scalable IAM solutions that adapt to the evolving needs of modern enterprises.

IAM Threat Intelligence and Behavioral Analysis using Machine Learning

Identity and Access Management (IAM) plays a critical role in cybersecurity by ensuring that users and systems authenticate securely, access resources appropriately, and operate within predefined security policies. However, traditional IAM solutions that rely on static rules and manual oversight are increasingly ineffective against evolving threats such as account takeovers, insider threats, privilege escalation, and advanced persistent threats (APTs). The integration of machine learning into IAM systems enhances security by enabling real-time threat intelligence, anomaly detection, and behavioral analysis. By leveraging artificial intelligence, organizations can automate identity risk assessments, detect unauthorized access attempts, and enforce dynamic access control measures based on user behavior patterns.

Machine learning-driven IAM threat intelligence involves collecting and analyzing vast amounts of identity-related data, including login patterns, access logs, authentication events, and privilege assignments. This data is processed using statistical models and neural networks to identify deviations from normal behavior that may indicate security threats. Unlike traditional rule-based systems that rely on predefined policies, machine learning models continuously adapt to evolving attack techniques by learning from historical data and detecting patterns that may not be explicitly defined in static access control policies.

Behavioral analysis is a core component of machine learning-powered IAM security. By monitoring user activity over time, IAM systems can establish behavioral baselines that define typical authentication habits, resource usage, and access privileges. When a deviation from the established pattern occurs, the system can trigger security alerts, enforce step-up authentication, or block suspicious activity. For example, if an employee who normally logs in from a corporate office suddenly attempts to access critical systems from an unfamiliar location, the IAM system can require multi-factor authentication (MFA) or deny access entirely based on the risk score.

One of the key applications of machine learning in IAM threat detection is anomaly detection in authentication events. Unusual login behaviors, such as accessing multiple accounts from the same IP address, using high-risk devices, or logging in at irregular hours, can indicate credential compromise or malicious activity. Machine learning algorithms such as unsupervised clustering, isolation forests, and autoencoders can be used to detect outliers in authentication logs, flagging potentially fraudulent activities before they escalate into security breaches.

Privilege escalation detection is another area where machine learning improves IAM security. Attackers often attempt to gain unauthorized administrative access by exploiting misconfigurations, leveraging stolen credentials, or executing privilege escalation attacks. Machine learning models trained on historical access patterns can detect unauthorized privilege changes by identifying deviations in role assignments, unexpected policy modifications, or anomalous permission grants. By integrating privilege escalation monitoring with IAM enforcement mechanisms, organizations can automatically revoke excessive privileges or require additional authorization before changes take effect.

Insider threats pose a significant risk to IAM security, as employees and contractors with legitimate access may misuse their privileges for malicious purposes. Traditional IAM policies struggle to detect subtle indicators of insider threats, but machine learning-based behavioral analysis can identify patterns of suspicious activity. For instance, an employee suddenly accessing large volumes of sensitive data, downloading confidential files outside normal working hours, or modifying access policies without prior authorization may be exhibiting signs of malicious intent. By correlating IAM logs with behavioral analytics, machine learning models can flag high-risk users and enable security teams to take proactive action.

IAM threat intelligence powered by machine learning also enhances phishing detection and credential compromise mitigation. Phishing attacks remain one of the most common methods used to steal user credentials, often leading to account takeovers and unauthorized access. Machine learning models can analyze email content, user behavior, and authentication logs to detect phishing attempts and compromised accounts. For example, if a user logs in from an unrecognized device after receiving a phishing email, the IAM system can require additional identity verification or temporarily restrict access until the login is verified.

Real-time IAM risk scoring is another critical application of machine learning in identity security. Instead of applying static access rules, organizations can use dynamic risk-based authentication to adjust security controls based on real-time threat assessments. Machine learning algorithms evaluate factors such as device fingerprinting, geolocation, behavioral trends, and historical access records to assign risk scores to authentication attempts. If a login attempt exceeds a predefined risk threshold, the IAM system can enforce stronger authentication measures, escalate to human review, or block access entirely.

IAM solutions that integrate machine learning-based threat intelligence can also leverage predictive analytics to anticipate security incidents before they occur. By analyzing historical attack data and user behavior trends, predictive models can identify high-risk users, vulnerable access policies, and potential security gaps. These insights enable organizations to proactively adjust IAM configurations, enforce least privilege principles, and strengthen authentication policies to reduce the likelihood of breaches.

Cloud IAM environments benefit significantly from machine learning-driven security enhancements. As organizations migrate to multi-cloud and hybrid environments, managing identities across distributed infrastructures becomes increasingly complex. Machine learning algorithms can help detect cross-cloud access anomalies, prevent lateral movement attacks, and enforce zero-trust security principles. Cloud-based IAM platforms such as AWS IAM, Microsoft Entra ID (formerly Azure Active Directory), and Google Cloud IAM incorporate AI-driven threat detection to analyze access patterns, detect anomalies, and automatically remediate security risks.

The integration of machine learning into IAM threat intelligence also improves compliance and auditability. Regulatory frameworks such as GDPR, HIPAA, and NIST 800-53 require organizations to maintain strong identity security controls and continuously monitor access activity. Machine learning-powered IAM analytics generate detailed audit trails, enabling organizations to demonstrate compliance with security standards. Automated reporting tools can provide real-time insights into identity risks, access violations, and policy enforcement trends, reducing the burden on security and compliance teams.

Implementing machine learning in IAM threat intelligence requires a robust data pipeline that collects, processes, and analyzes identity-related events. Organizations must aggregate authentication logs, access policies, privilege assignments, and user behavior data from multiple sources, including SIEM (Security Information and Event Management) platforms, identity providers, and endpoint security solutions. This data is then fed into machine learning models that continuously learn from new identity interactions and refine their threat detection capabilities.

Despite its advantages, machine learning in IAM security also presents challenges. False positives and false negatives can impact the accuracy of threat detection models, leading to unnecessary access restrictions or undetected security breaches. To mitigate this, organizations must fine-tune machine learning models, implement feedback loops, and incorporate human review mechanisms to validate security alerts. Additionally, adversarial machine learning threats, where attackers attempt to manipulate AI-driven security models, must be addressed through robust model validation and anomaly detection techniques.

As cyber threats continue to evolve, machine learning-driven IAM threat intelligence and behavioral analysis will play an increasingly vital role in protecting digital identities and securing access to enterprise resources. By leveraging AI-powered security analytics, organizations can detect identity threats in real time, enforce adaptive authentication policies, and strengthen IAM defenses against sophisticated attacks.

Reverse Engineering IAM Systems for Penetration Testing and Red Teaming

Identity and Access Management (IAM) systems serve as the backbone of enterprise security, governing authentication, authorization, and access control policies. However, despite their critical role, IAM systems are often targeted by attackers seeking to escalate privileges, exfiltrate sensitive data, or move laterally within an organization's infrastructure. Penetration testers and red teams must thoroughly assess IAM implementations to uncover vulnerabilities, misconfigurations, and security gaps before malicious actors can exploit them. Reverse engineering IAM systems enables security professionals to analyze authentication mechanisms, privilege structures, token issuance workflows, and access policies to identify weaknesses that could lead to compromise.

The process of reverse engineering IAM systems begins with reconnaissance, where testers gather intelligence on identity management frameworks, authentication mechanisms, and user provisioning processes. Open-source intelligence (OSINT) techniques can be used to discover exposed IAM-related endpoints, publicly accessible APIs, leaked credentials, and metadata about the organization's IAM architecture. External reconnaissance tools such as Shodan and Censys help identify cloud identity endpoints, Single Sign-On (SSO) implementations, and identity federation configurations that may be susceptible to attack. Internally, red teams use network sniffing, DNS enumeration, and metadata extraction to map out IAM components within an enterprise environment.

Once reconnaissance is complete, penetration testers move to analyzing authentication mechanisms. Most modern IAM systems rely on protocols such as OAuth 2.0, OpenID Connect (OIDC), Security Assertion Markup Language (SAML), Kerberos, or Lightweight Directory Access Protocol (LDAP) for authentication and identity federation. Each of these protocols presents unique attack surfaces. OAuth and OIDC implementations are commonly targeted for misconfigured redirect URIs, token leakage, weak client authentication, and session hijacking vulnerabilities. SAML-based SSO deployments are prone to XML signature wrapping attacks, unsigned assertions, and insecure token relay mechanisms. Penetration testers use tools such as SAML Raider, Burp Suite, and jwt_tool to analyze token structures, manipulate authentication flows, and attempt token forgery attacks.

Password-based authentication remains one of the weakest links in IAM security. Red teams attempt brute-force and credential stuffing attacks against login portals, exploiting weak or reused passwords. Tools like Hydra, Medusa, and Patator automate login attempts against IAM endpoints, testing common password patterns and leaked credential databases. Multi-factor authentication (MFA) implementations are assessed for bypass techniques, such as exploiting SMS-based MFA through SIM swapping, session hijacking, or man-in-the-middle (MITM) attacks. Attackers also analyze authentication logs to identify users who have not enabled MFA, providing easier targets for account takeovers.

Session management flaws in IAM systems provide another attack vector. If session tokens are not properly invalidated upon logout or privilege revocation, attackers can exploit session fixation or token replay attacks. Penetration testers analyze how IAM solutions handle session expiration, token rotation, and refresh token policies. Tools like jwt_tool and OAuth2 Proxy help security professionals manipulate JWTs and OAuth access tokens, testing whether token expiration policies are properly enforced and whether session hijacking is possible.

Privilege escalation is a primary objective in IAM red teaming exercises. Attackers seek to exploit overprivileged accounts, excessive role assignments, and insecure IAM policies to escalate their privileges within an environment. Cloud IAM implementations in AWS, Azure, and Google Cloud are commonly targeted for misconfigured IAM roles, insecure cross-account access policies, and overly permissive identity federation settings. Tools like CloudSplaining, PMapper, and AWS IAM Access Analyzer help penetration testers visualize privilege relationships and detect role misconfigurations that allow privilege escalation.

Active Directory (AD) environments are particularly susceptible to privilege escalation attacks if misconfigurations exist in Group Policy Objects (GPOs), Kerberos ticketing, or password policies. Red teams use BloodHound, SharpHound, and Mimikatz to enumerate AD privilege structures, identify weak Kerberos service tickets (Kerberoasting), and extract NTLM hashes from memory. Attackers also analyze AD replication permissions for DCShadow attacks, where rogue domain controllers inject malicious identity changes into AD.

IAM red teaming also involves identity persistence techniques, where attackers establish long-term access to compromised accounts. Persistence can be achieved by creating new IAM roles, modifying authentication policies, injecting rogue SAML assertions, or modifying MFA settings to lock out legitimate users. In cloud environments, adversaries often create long-lived API keys, exploit IAM trust relationships, or modify service account permissions to maintain hidden access even after initial compromise. Security teams must audit IAM logs continuously to detect unauthorized identity modifications and privilege escalation attempts.

Social engineering attacks complement technical IAM penetration testing by targeting identity verification weaknesses. Red teams simulate phishing attacks to harvest authentication credentials, trick users into approving rogue MFA requests, or exploit weak password reset policies. Common phishing techniques include credential interception via reverse proxies (Evilginx2), OAuth consent phishing, and malicious SAML login prompts that impersonate legitimate identity providers. Effective IAM security requires training employees to recognize phishing attempts and enforcing phishing-resistant authentication methods such as WebAuthn or FIDO2-based security keys.

IAM system misconfigurations often expose sensitive API endpoints, where attackers can extract user directory data, authentication logs, or privileged role assignments. API security testing involves analyzing IAM APIs for missing authentication headers, insecure API keys, token leakage, and unauthorized data exposure. Tools like Postman, Burp Suite, and ZAP Proxy help penetration testers enumerate IAM API endpoints, modify authentication tokens, and inject malicious payloads to bypass access controls.

Logging and monitoring weaknesses in IAM implementations can allow attackers to operate undetected. Penetration testers assess whether identity-related security events are properly logged, including failed login attempts, privilege changes, and suspicious session activity. Security Information and Event Management (SIEM) solutions such as Splunk, Elastic Security, and Microsoft Sentinel should aggregate IAM logs and trigger alerts for abnormal access patterns. If IAM logging is misconfigured, attackers can cover their tracks by deleting logs, disabling audit policies, or injecting false identity events to mislead security teams.

To defend against IAM threats, organizations must conduct continuous penetration testing, perform regular IAM audits, enforce least privilege access policies, and implement Zero Trust IAM frameworks. Automated IAM policy analysis, adaptive authentication, and identity behavior analytics enhance detection and prevention mechanisms. Red teaming exercises provide critical insights into real-world attack scenarios, enabling security teams to harden IAM defenses and reduce the risk of identity compromise.

Securing IAM Microservices using mTLS, SPIFFE, and Istio Policies

As modern applications increasingly adopt microservices architectures, securing Identity and Access Management (IAM) components within these distributed environments becomes critical. Traditional IAM security models rely on centralized authentication and authorization mechanisms, but microservices architectures introduce new challenges, including service-to-service authentication, dynamic identity management, and zero-trust security enforcement. To address these challenges, mutual Transport Layer Security (mTLS), Secure Production Identity Framework for Everyone (SPIFFE), and Istio service mesh policies provide a robust approach for securing IAM microservices. These technologies ensure that authentication, authorization, and encryption are enforced consistently across microservices, protecting identity data and preventing unauthorized access.

Mutual TLS (mTLS) is a fundamental security mechanism that ensures encrypted communication and mutual authentication between microservices. Unlike traditional TLS, which only verifies the identity of the server, mTLS requires both the client and server to present cryptographic certificates, establishing trust before communication is allowed. In IAM microservices, mTLS is essential for securing API requests, preventing unauthorized access, and protecting sensitive identity transactions. By enforcing mTLS, organizations can eliminate reliance on shared secrets, API keys, or token-based authentication between internal services, reducing the risk of credential leaks and man-in-the-middle attacks.

Implementing mTLS in microservices involves generating and managing X.509 certificates for each service, ensuring that only trusted services can communicate. Certificate authorities (CAs) issue service identities, which are used to authenticate microservices dynamically. Automated certificate rotation and renewal mechanisms prevent stale or compromised certificates from being used. In Kubernetes-based environments, Istio provides built-in support for mTLS, enabling automatic certificate issuance, renewal, and validation without requiring changes to application code. By configuring Istio to enforce mTLS at the service mesh level, IAM microservices can securely authenticate each other without relying on external authentication providers.

SPIFFE (Secure Production Identity Framework for Everyone) is an open standard that defines how microservices authenticate and establish trust within distributed environments. SPIFFE provides a standardized identity framework that eliminates the need for long-lived credentials, enabling microservices to securely authenticate using dynamic workload identities. Instead of using API keys or traditional authentication tokens, SPIFFE assigns each service a SPIFFE ID, a cryptographic identity that uniquely identifies workloads in a zero-trust architecture.

In an IAM microservices environment, SPIFFE simplifies identity management by providing a secure, scalable, and automated way to assign identities to microservices. Workload identities are dynamically issued using SPIFFE Verifiable Identity Documents (SVIDs), which act as cryptographic proof of service identity. These identities are then used for mutual authentication, ensuring that only authorized microservices can access IAM services such as authentication, user provisioning, and policy enforcement. SPIFFE integrates seamlessly with service meshes like Istio, providing an additional layer of security by binding service identities to dynamically generated certificates.

Istio service mesh enhances IAM microservices security by providing policy-based access control, observability, and workload encryption. By using Istio, organizations can enforce fine-grained authentication and authorization policies without modifying application code. Istio enables zero-trust networking by default, ensuring that all microservices interactions are authenticated, encrypted, and authorized based on predefined security policies.

One of the key security features of Istio is Authorization Policies, which define rules governing access to microservices based on identity, role, or attributes. IAM microservices can use Istio Authorization Policies to restrict access to identity-related APIs, ensuring that only authorized services or users can perform authentication, authorization, or identity management operations. For example, an Istio policy can enforce that only specific IAM microservices are allowed to query user credentials, preventing unauthorized services from accessing sensitive identity data.

Istio's RequestAuthentication policies allow IAM microservices to verify JWT tokens, ensuring that API requests include valid, signed identity tokens before granting access. By integrating Istio with an identity provider (IdP) such as Microsoft Entra ID, Okta, or Google Cloud IAM, IAM microservices can validate OAuth 2.0 and OpenID Connect (OIDC) tokens at the network layer, reducing the risk of token replay attacks. Istio's PeerAuthentication policies extend this security model by enforcing mTLS between microservices, ensuring encrypted service-to-service communication and preventing eavesdropping.

Istio's observability features, such as telemetry, logging, and distributed tracing, provide visibility into IAM microservices authentication and authorization workflows. By integrating Istio with Prometheus, Grafana, and Jaeger, security teams can monitor IAM service interactions, detect anomalies, and analyze authentication failures in real-time. Monitoring IAM-related traffic within the service mesh helps detect unauthorized access attempts, privilege escalation attempts, and unusual authentication patterns that may indicate a security breach.

Another advantage of using Istio for IAM microservices security is service segmentation. In a microservices environment, not all services require access to identity management APIs. Istio's NetworkPolicies and ServiceEntry configurations enable organizations to segment IAM services, restricting access based on namespaces, labels, or authentication policies. This approach minimizes the attack surface by ensuring that only authorized services can interact with IAM components, preventing lateral movement attacks.

IAM microservices deployed in hybrid or multi-cloud environments benefit from Istio's cross-cluster security policies, which enforce authentication and authorization controls across different cloud providers. By leveraging federated SPIFFE identities, IAM microservices running in different cloud environments can establish trust without relying on cloud-specific identity solutions. This approach enables organizations to maintain consistent IAM security policies across AWS, Azure, and Google Cloud, ensuring that service-to-service authentication and access controls remain uniform.

Security best practices for implementing mTLS, SPIFFE, and Istio in IAM microservices include enforcing short-lived credentials, automating certificate rotation, and implementing least privilege access control for service identities. Organizations should regularly audit IAM microservices permissions, review Istio access logs, and implement risk-based authentication policies that dynamically adjust security requirements based on threat intelligence and user behavior analysis.

Zero-trust IAM architectures built on mTLS, SPIFFE, and Istio policies enhance microservices security by eliminating implicit trust between workloads, enforcing strong authentication and encryption, and preventing unauthorized access to identity-related services. These technologies provide a scalable, automated, and policy-driven approach to securing IAM microservices, ensuring that authentication, authorization, and identity federation workflows remain protected in dynamic cloud-native environments.

Advanced RBAC & ABAC Implementations with Dynamic Attribute Resolution

Role-Based Access Control (RBAC) and Attribute-Based Access Control (ABAC) are two of the most widely adopted access control models in modern Identity and Access Management (IAM) systems. RBAC assigns permissions to users based on predefined roles, while ABAC enhances this approach by incorporating dynamic attributes such as user identity, device information, location, and time of access. As enterprises move toward highly scalable and adaptable security frameworks, advanced implementations of RBAC and ABAC with dynamic attribute resolution provide more granular, context-aware access control policies that improve security while maintaining flexibility.

RBAC remains a fundamental access control model for many organizations due to its simplicity and ease of management. Users are assigned to roles, and these roles dictate the permissions granted within a system. However, traditional RBAC suffers from role explosion, where an excessive number of roles must be created to cover all possible access scenarios. To mitigate this, organizations implement hierarchical RBAC, which introduces role inheritance, reducing redundancy by allowing higher-level roles to automatically inherit permissions from lower-level roles. Additionally, constraint-based RBAC enhances security by applying dynamic conditions such as temporal access limits, geographic restrictions, and device-based authentication before granting access.

ABAC extends RBAC by evaluating a wide range of attributes before making access decisions. Instead of relying solely on roles, ABAC policies consider user attributes (e.g., department, job title, security clearance), environmental attributes (e.g., IP address, location, network risk score), resource attributes (e.g., file sensitivity level, database classification), and action attributes (e.g., read, write, delete). This flexible model enables fine-grained access control without the need for extensive role definitions. For example, an ABAC policy might allow employees in the finance department to access payroll data only if they are physically located in a corporate office and using a trusted device.

Dynamic attribute resolution is a key component of advanced RBAC and ABAC implementations. Instead of relying on static attributes stored in identity directories, IAM systems must dynamically fetch and evaluate attributes in real time. This is achieved through integrations with external data sources such as Security Information and Event Management (SIEM) systems, Threat Intelligence Platforms, Risk Engines, and Device Trust Services. When a user attempts to access a resource, the IAM system queries these sources to obtain up-to-date context, ensuring that access decisions reflect the latest security conditions.

One of the primary use cases for dynamic attribute resolution is risk-based access control (RBAC with risk awareness). Traditional RBAC assumes that all users within a role should have identical access rights, but this does not account for real-time risk factors. By integrating with risk engines, organizations can enforce adaptive role elevation, where users may be granted temporary elevated privileges if their risk level is low. For example, an administrator may be granted emergency access to production systems only if their login originates from a known corporate network and their behavior does not exhibit anomalies. If an elevated risk is detected, additional authentication factors (such as MFA or identity verification) may be required before access is granted.

ABAC implementations with dynamic attribute resolution also enable policy-driven Just-In-Time (JIT) access. Instead of granting persistent access to users based on predefined roles, policies evaluate attributes at the time of access and dynamically determine whether access should be granted. This approach is particularly useful in zero-trust security models, where default access is denied unless explicitly permitted based on context. For instance, a cloud administrator may be allowed to modify network configurations only if their identity is verified, their endpoint complies with security policies, and the requested action aligns with their usual behavior patterns.

Implementing advanced RBAC and ABAC requires a policy enforcement engine (PEP) capable of interpreting and enforcing complex policies. IAM systems integrate with policy decision points (PDPs) that evaluate attribute-based rules against real-time user requests. Standardized policy languages such as XACML (eXtensible Access Control Markup Language) and Rego (used in Open Policy Agent - OPA) provide a structured way to define and enforce ABAC policies. These languages allow IAM architects to write policies that incorporate conditions, environmental factors, and temporal constraints.

For large-scale enterprises, RBAC-ABAC hybrid models provide a balanced approach that combines the best aspects of both models. Users are assigned roles that define baseline access, but additional attribute-based conditions refine these permissions dynamically. A role-plus-attributes model prevents excessive role creation while allowing granular access control. For example, all software engineers might be assigned a "developer" role that grants them basic access to development resources, but ABAC rules further restrict access based on project assignments, security clearance, or the sensitivity of the data being accessed.

Advanced IAM implementations also integrate with cloud-native access control frameworks such as AWS IAM Policies, Azure

Conditional Access Policies, and Google Cloud IAM Conditions. These platforms allow administrators to define dynamic access policies that evaluate real-time attributes. AWS IAM, for example, supports attribute-based access control through IAM conditions, which enforce access rules based on IP ranges, resource tags, and authentication context. Similarly, Azure Conditional Access enables adaptive access control policies that require step-up authentication when users attempt to access high-risk applications from untrusted networks.

Security and compliance considerations play a major role in dynamic RBAC and ABAC implementations. Regulations such as GDPR, HIPAA, and NIST 800-53 require organizations to enforce least privilege access, continuously monitor identity activities, and implement fine-grained access controls. By leveraging real-time attribute evaluation and risk-aware policies, organizations can comply with these standards while reducing insider threats and unauthorized access incidents. Audit logs and access review mechanisms further enhance compliance by providing detailed records of access requests, attribute evaluations, and policy enforcement decisions.

Performance optimization is another critical factor when implementing dynamic access control models. Attribute evaluation at scale requires efficient caching strategies, API rate limiting, and optimized database queries to prevent latency in authentication workflows. Large enterprises deploy distributed policy engines that cache frequently used attributes and precompute access decisions to reduce processing overhead. Additionally, edge computing architectures allow ABAC policies to be enforced closer to the user, minimizing latency in distributed environments.

As organizations transition to zero-trust architectures, RBAC and ABAC must evolve to support continuous authentication and real-time authorization adjustments. By integrating with User and Entity Behavior Analytics (UEBA) and Artificial Intelligence-driven Identity Analytics, IAM systems can dynamically adjust access levels based on emerging threats and behavioral anomalies. This ensures that access policies remain adaptive, resilient, and aligned with an organization's security posture.

Advanced RBAC and ABAC implementations with dynamic attribute resolution provide organizations with scalable, adaptive, and policy-driven access control. By leveraging real-time context, integrating with external security intelligence sources, and enforcing zero-trust principles, organizations can enhance security while maintaining the flexibility needed to support dynamic business environments.

Developing IAM SDKs and Libraries for Enterprise Identity Integrations

Enterprise Identity and Access Management (IAM) requires seamless integration across various applications, cloud services, and on-premises systems. Organizations rely on IAM solutions to enforce authentication, authorization, user provisioning, and security policies consistently across their IT ecosystems. To facilitate these integrations, developers build IAM Software Development Kits (SDKs) and libraries that abstract complex identity processes, provide reusable authentication and authorization components, and ensure compliance with security best practices. Developing robust IAM SDKs involves implementing secure authentication flows, token management, role-based access control (RBAC), and federation protocols while maintaining performance, scalability, and usability.

IAM SDKs serve as an abstraction layer that simplifies interactions with identity providers (IdPs), authentication protocols, and access control mechanisms. Instead of requiring developers to implement identity flows manually, SDKs provide pre-built modules that handle user authentication, secure token exchange, session management, and policy enforcement. These libraries enable applications to authenticate users against enterprise IAM platforms such as Microsoft Entra ID, Okta, Autho, Google Cloud IAM, and AWS Cognito without deep knowledge of the underlying protocols.

A well-designed IAM SDK must support industry-standard authentication protocols, including OAuth 2.0, OpenID Connect (OIDC), Security Assertion Markup Language (SAML), and Kerberos. Each protocol has unique requirements, and the SDK must abstract these complexities while providing a unified API for developers. OAuth 2.0-based SDKs must handle authorization flows such as authorization code flow, implicit flow, client credentials flow, and device authorization flow. OIDC support must include ID token validation, user claims retrieval, and session management to ensure secure authentication. SDKs designed for SAML must implement assertion validation, metadata parsing, and signature verification, enabling federated identity integrations with enterprise applications.

Token management is a critical aspect of IAM SDKs, ensuring that authentication and authorization tokens are securely issued, validated, stored, and refreshed. Secure token handling involves validating JWT signatures, checking expiration claims, and managing token storage securely to prevent token leakage. SDKs must support token introspection for verifying access tokens in real time and automatic token refresh mechanisms to maintain seamless authentication without requiring user re-login. Secure storage of refresh tokens must leverage platform-specific secure stores such as Android Keystore, iOS Keychain, and secure hardware modules to prevent unauthorized access.

IAM SDKs must also facilitate role-based access control (RBAC) and attribute-based access control (ABAC) by providing APIs that retrieve user roles, permissions, and contextual attributes. Applications integrating with IAM SDKs should be able to determine whether a user has the necessary permissions before executing privileged operations. SDKs implementing fine-grained authorization policies must support policy-based access control (PBAC) by evaluating user attributes, environmental conditions, and policy rules dynamically. Integration with policy engines such as Open Policy Agent (OPA) allows IAM SDKs to enforce complex authorization decisions based on predefined security policies.

Enterprise applications often require single sign-on (SSO) capabilities, enabling users to authenticate once and access multiple services without repeated logins. IAM SDKs designed for SSO must support federated authentication using SAML, OAuth 2.0/OIDC, and WS-Federation, allowing applications to integrate with corporate identity providers. SSO SDKs must handle session management, token revocation, and identity federation workflows, ensuring that authentication sessions are securely maintained across services while preventing session hijacking and unauthorized token reuse.

Cross-platform support is essential for IAM SDKs, as enterprise applications span multiple operating systems, frameworks, and development environments. SDKs must provide language-specific implementations for Java, Python, JavaScript (Node.js and frontend frameworks like React and Angular), .NET, Go, and mobile platforms such as Swift (iOS) and Kotlin (Android). By providing well-documented SDKs, RESTful APIs, and GraphQL endpoints, IAM libraries ensure that developers can integrate identity services into any application stack seamlessly.

Secure API design is a fundamental principle in IAM SDK development. SDKs must implement zero-trust security principles by ensuring that every request is authenticated, authorized, and validated before processing. Secure SDK implementations should enforce mutual TLS (mTLS), OAuth proof-of-possession tokens, and secure secret storage to prevent API key leaks and unauthorized access. Additionally, IAM SDKs should encrypt all sensitive data in transit using TLS 1.2+ and enforce strong cryptographic hashing for password storage using PBKDF2, Argon2, or bcrypt.

IAM SDKs must also provide audit logging and monitoring capabilities, enabling security teams to track authentication events, access control violations, and anomalous behavior. SDKs should generate structured logs for authentication attempts, failed logins, token usage, and role modifications, which can be forwarded to Security Information and Event Management (SIEM) platforms for real-time monitoring and incident response. Logging frameworks should support JSON-based log formats, log integrity verification, and log anonymization to comply with regulatory requirements such as GDPR and HIPAA.

Performance optimization in IAM SDKs is essential to minimize authentication latency and improve application responsiveness. SDKs must cache frequently used identity attributes, optimize API calls using batch requests, and support asynchronous authentication flows to reduce blocking operations. SDKs integrating with content delivery networks (CDNs) and edge authentication proxies can further enhance performance by reducing the need for repeated authentication requests to centralized identity providers.

Enterprise IAM SDKs must also integrate with multi-factor authentication (MFA) providers, enabling applications to enforce additional authentication layers beyond passwords. SDKs should support TOTP (Time-based One-Time Passwords), push notifications, hardware security keys (FIDO2/WebAuthn), and biometric authentication. MFA enforcement must be flexible, allowing developers to implement adaptive authentication workflows that require step-up authentication based on user risk levels, device trust, or location anomalies.

IAM SDK testing and security validation must be an integral part of the development lifecycle. SDKs must undergo penetration testing, static code analysis, dependency vulnerability scanning, and fuzz testing to detect security flaws before deployment. Secure Software Development Lifecycle (SSDLC) practices must be followed, ensuring that IAM SDKs meet OWASP Application Security Verification Standard (ASVS) guidelines and CWE (Common Weakness Enumeration) security best practices.

As organizations transition to cloud-native IAM architectures, SDKs must support serverless authentication workflows, enabling seamless integration with AWS Lambda, Azure Functions, and Google Cloud Functions. Cloud-native IAM SDKs must be designed for event-driven architectures, ensuring that authentication and access control decisions can be dynamically enforced in microservices, Kubernetes clusters, and API gateways.

Developing robust IAM SDKs and libraries requires a balance between security, usability, and performance. By providing secure authentication flows, flexible authorization mechanisms, cross-platform support, and compliance-ready security policies, IAM SDKs empower enterprises to integrate identity services efficiently while maintaining high-security standards. Well-designed SDKs streamline identity integrations, reduce development effort, and ensure that applications enforce consistent and scalable identity security across all enterprise systems.

Extending IAM Solutions using Plugins and Custom Modules (Okta Hooks, SailPoint Rules, ForgeRock Scripting)

Identity and Access Management (IAM) platforms provide out-of-the-box functionality for authentication, authorization, user provisioning, and compliance enforcement. However, enterprises often require customized identity workflows, integration with legacy applications, or specialized security policies that extend beyond standard IAM capabilities. To address these requirements, leading IAM solutions such as Okta, SailPoint, and ForgeRock allow developers to extend their platforms using plugins, custom modules, and scripting frameworks. By leveraging Okta Hooks, SailPoint Rules, and ForgeRock scripting, organizations can implement tailored identity operations, automate security policies, and integrate IAM solutions seamlessly with business processes.

Okta provides a powerful extension framework through Okta Hooks, allowing developers to insert custom logic into authentication, user lifecycle events, and authorization decisions. Inline Hooks in Okta enable organizations to modify authentication and authorization responses dynamically. For example, when a user logs in, an Inline Hook can call an external API to check risk scores before allowing access. Similarly, Event Hooks notify external systems when specific IAM events occur, such as user deactivation or role changes, enabling real-time synchronization with HR systems or security monitoring tools.

Customizing Okta authentication workflows often involves modifying OAuth 2.0 and OpenID Connect (OIDC) token issuance policies. Using Inline Token Hooks, organizations can enrich identity tokens with additional claims, such as user risk assessments or contextual security attributes. This allows downstream applications to enforce risk-based authentication policies by evaluating enhanced token payloads. Additionally, Registration Hooks enable validation of user data during self-service registration, enforcing compliance checks before creating accounts.

SailPoint IdentityIQ, a leading identity governance and administration (IGA) platform, supports extensibility through SailPoint Rules and custom Java-based scripts. Lifecycle Event Rules allow organizations to define custom workflows for user onboarding, role assignments, and deprovisioning. For example, when a new employee joins the organization, a Create Identity Rule can trigger a workflow that assigns default access permissions based on job function, department, and geographic location.

SailPoint also enables automated access reviews and policy enforcement using Policy Rules. Organizations can implement dynamic segregation-of-duties (SoD) checks that prevent conflicting role assignments. For instance, if a user is granted access to both financial approval and payment processing systems, a Custom Policy Rule can flag the access request for manual review. Identity Refresh Rules help synchronize user attributes between SailPoint and external directories, ensuring that identity data remains consistent across multiple identity stores.

For custom connectors and provisioning workflows, SailPoint supports Application Rules that define custom attribute mappings, transformation logic, and access request validations. These rules are essential when integrating with legacy applications or non-standard identity sources, allowing organizations to tailor identity synchronization processes based on business logic. Scripted Identity Mappings further enhance flexibility by allowing developers to define conditional attribute transformations, such as generating unique usernames based on complex business naming conventions.

ForgeRock, a comprehensive IAM and identity federation platform, provides an extensive scripting framework for custom authentication modules, policy evaluation, and access control enforcement. ForgeRock's Authentication Trees allow developers to insert custom nodes using JavaScript or Groovy scripting. This enables organizations to implement adaptive authentication workflows, where authentication strength dynamically adjusts based on user risk levels, device posture, or geolocation.

For advanced authentication scenarios, ForgeRock's Custom Scripted Decision Nodes provide programmatic control over login processes.

Developers can define authentication flows that query external threat intelligence platforms, validate digital signatures, or enforce biometric verification before allowing access. ForgeRock also supports custom OAuth 2.0 grant handlers, allowing organizations to define fine-grained access token issuance policies based on enterprise security requirements.

Extending ForgeRock's authorization policies involves scripting custom conditions in policy decision points (PDPs). Using Groovy-based Policy Condition Scripts, organizations can define attribute-based access control (ABAC) rules that evaluate user risk scores, session attributes, or transaction details in real-time. This enables the implementation of context-aware authorization policies, where access to sensitive resources is granted only when specific security conditions are met.

For identity federation and cross-domain authentication, ForgeRock allows custom SAML attribute processing scripts that transform identity assertions before passing them to service providers. These scripts enable dynamic claim augmentation, where additional security attributes such as device reputation, last login timestamps, and compliance statuses are injected into identity assertions to enhance downstream authorization policies.

Integrating IAM solutions with cloud-native architectures and DevSecOps pipelines requires automation through plugins and scripting. Okta, SailPoint, and ForgeRock all support API-driven extensibility, allowing organizations to build CI/CD pipelines for identity governance, automate role-based access control (RBAC) assignments, and enforce IAM security policies programmatically. By leveraging serverless computing platforms such as AWS Lambda, Azure Functions, and Google Cloud Functions, organizations can create event-driven IAM workflows that execute real-time identity synchronization, security audits, and access revocation based on IAM event triggers.

Security best practices for extending IAM solutions involve enforcing least privilege access, ensuring code integrity in custom scripts, and performing continuous security validation of IAM extensions. Developers must implement secure API interactions, validate input data rigorously, and prevent unauthorized script execution within IAM platforms. By adopting role-based script execution controls and enforcing cryptographic signing of custom modules, organizations can mitigate the risk of identity-based attacks resulting from malicious IAM extensions.

Extending IAM solutions using plugins, custom modules, and scripting frameworks provides organizations with the flexibility to tailor identity workflows, enforce security policies dynamically, and integrate with complex enterprise ecosystems. Whether through Okta Hooks, SailPoint Rules, or ForgeRock scripting, organizations can build scalable, secure, and adaptive IAM solutions that align with evolving business and security requirements.

Enterprise Session Management: JWT, OAuth DPoP, and Refresh Token Strategies

Session management is a critical component of Identity and Access Management (IAM) in enterprise environments, ensuring that authenticated users maintain secure and efficient access to protected resources while preventing unauthorized access. Traditional session management relied on server-side session storage, but modern distributed and cloud-based architectures demand scalable, stateless authentication mechanisms. JSON Web Tokens (JWT), OAuth 2.0 Demonstration of Proof-of-Possession (DPoP), and refresh token strategies provide robust solutions for managing authentication sessions while balancing security, scalability, and performance.

JWTs have become the de facto standard for stateless authentication in enterprise IAM due to their compact, self-contained structure and cryptographic integrity. Unlike traditional session IDs stored on servers, JWTs encapsulate authentication claims, expiration times, and cryptographic signatures, allowing authentication to be verified without querying a central session store. A standard JWT consists of three parts: a header (specifying the signing algorithm), a payload (containing user claims and session metadata), and a signature (ensuring token integrity and authenticity). This structure enables JWTs to be securely transmitted across microservices, cloud applications, and API gateways without requiring continuous backend lookups.

Despite their advantages, JWTs introduce security challenges if not properly managed. Because JWTs are self-contained, revoking a compromised JWT before its expiration is difficult unless additional token management mechanisms are implemented. To mitigate this, enterprises adopt short-lived JWTs combined with refresh token workflows, ensuring that authentication sessions remain active without exposing long-lived tokens.

OAuth 2.0 introduces refresh tokens as a secure mechanism to extend authentication sessions without requiring users to reauthenticate frequently. Unlike access tokens, which have short expiration times, refresh tokens allow clients to request new access tokens without user interaction. The OAuth 2.0 flow ensures that refresh tokens remain confidential, are stored securely by clients, and are not exposed in API requests. A properly implemented refresh token strategy reduces the risk of session hijacking and prevents the need for persistent JWTs with extended expiration periods.

To further enhance security, refresh token rotation policies prevent token reuse attacks. When a client requests a new access token, the previous refresh token is invalidated, and a new one is issued. This prevents attackers from using stolen refresh tokens, as they become invalid once a new one is generated. Additionally, refresh tokens should have a maximum lifespan, requiring periodic reauthentication to prevent long-term compromise. Implementing client binding ensures that refresh tokens can only be used by the specific device or client that initially requested them, reducing the risk of stolen token reuse.

OAuth 2.0 Demonstration of Proof-of-Possession (DPoP) enhances session security by binding access tokens to a specific client instance, preventing token replay attacks. Traditional OAuth 2.0 bearer tokens can be stolen and reused by attackers if intercepted in transit. DPoP mitigates this risk by requiring clients to generate cryptographic proofs with each request. This proof consists of a signed JWT containing the HTTP method, requested resource URL, and a unique nonce, ensuring that tokens cannot be reused outside their original request context.

DPoP ensures that even if an access token is exposed, it cannot be used by unauthorized parties without the original client's private key. This provides additional protection against man-in-the-middle (MITM) attacks and credential stuffing. Enterprises integrating DPoP into their OAuth flows must manage key storage securely using hardware-backed keystores, ensuring that proof-of-possession keys are not extracted from client devices.

Enterprise session management also requires adaptive token expiration policies to balance security and user experience. High-risk access scenarios, such as authentication from untrusted devices or locations, should enforce shorter token expiration times and require step-up authentication. Risk-based session management allows organizations to dynamically adjust session durations based on user behavior, device trust scores, and authentication context.

To prevent session fixation attacks, enterprises must implement session binding mechanisms, ensuring that tokens are only valid when used from the originally authenticated device. Device-bound tokens leverage device fingerprints, hardware security modules (HSMs), or WebAuthn cryptographic attestations to restrict token usage to specific environments. Additionally, session hijacking can be mitigated by enforcing strict IP binding policies, detecting sudden geographic changes in authentication sessions, and requiring reauthentication when risk thresholds are exceeded.

Enterprise applications must implement secure token storage practices to prevent unauthorized access to JWTs, refresh tokens, and DPoP private keys. Browser-based applications should never store tokens in local storage or session storage, as these mechanisms are vulnerable to cross-site scripting (XSS) attacks. Instead, HTTP-only, secure cookies should be used for token storage, ensuring that authentication tokens are inaccessible to JavaScript execution. For mobile applications, encrypted keychain storage (iOS Keychain, Android Keystore) prevents unauthorized token access.

Session termination and revocation play a key role in IAM security. OAuth 2.0 lacks a native token revocation mechanism for JWTs, requiring enterprises to maintain token blacklists, leverage introspection endpoints, or use revocable token identifiers.

Centralized session revocation services enable IAM platforms to revoke access tokens across multiple applications in real time, forcing users to reauthenticate upon detecting compromise or session anomalies. WebSockets and push notification mechanisms allow IAM platforms to notify client applications when tokens become invalid, preventing unauthorized continued use of compromised sessions.

For organizations adopting multi-cloud IAM strategies, session management must seamlessly integrate with identity providers such as Microsoft Entra ID, Okta, Autho, and AWS Cognito. Multi-cloud environments require federated session management, ensuring that authentication sessions persist across identity domains while enforcing consistent security policies. Cross-cloud session management frameworks leverage OIDC session management endpoints to synchronize authentication states between cloud providers, ensuring that users experience seamless sign-on across enterprise applications.

Logging and monitoring are essential components of secure session management, providing visibility into authentication events, token exchanges, refresh attempts, and suspicious session behaviors. Security teams must implement real-time anomaly detection, flagging unauthorized refresh token use, multiple access attempts from different locations, and sudden spikes in token requests. Integration with SIEM platforms (Splunk, ELK, Azure Sentinel) enables centralized monitoring of IAM session logs, ensuring compliance with security regulations such as GDPR, HIPAA, and NIST 800-63.

Zero-trust IAM architectures enhance session security by enforcing continuous authentication, requiring periodic user revalidation based on session behavior, security posture, and AI-driven risk analysis. Instead of treating authentication as a one-time event, adaptive session enforcement ensures that access decisions remain dynamic throughout the user's session. By leveraging machine learning-driven IAM analytics, enterprises can identify and mitigate session anomalies, token abuse, and privilege escalation attempts before they result in security breaches.

By implementing JWT-based authentication, OAuth DPoP proof-of-possession mechanisms, refresh token rotation, and risk-based session policies, enterprises can build secure, scalable, and adaptive session management frameworks that protect user identities while ensuring seamless access to applications across distributed environments.

Building a Distributed Identity Verification System using Blockchain and Self-Sovereign Identity (SSI)

Identity verification is a fundamental requirement in digital interactions, ensuring that users, devices, and services can prove their legitimacy while maintaining security and privacy. Traditional identity verification relies on centralized authorities, such as governments, enterprises, and identity providers, which act as gatekeepers for authentication and authorization. However, these centralized models introduce risks related to data breaches, identity theft, lack of user control, and inefficiencies in cross-domain identity verification. To address these challenges, decentralized identity solutions leveraging blockchain technology and Self-Sovereign Identity (SSI) provide a scalable, secure, and privacy-enhancing approach to identity verification.

Blockchain-based identity verification shifts control from centralized authorities to a decentralized, cryptographically secure model where users retain ownership of their identity attributes. Unlike traditional IAM systems that rely on directory services or federated identity providers, SSI frameworks allow individuals and entities to manage their identity credentials without relying on intermediaries. Blockchain serves as the trust layer that verifies and records cryptographic proofs, ensuring immutability, transparency, and tamper resistance while preserving user privacy.

A distributed identity verification system using SSI and blockchain consists of issuers, holders, and verifiers, each playing a critical role in identity transactions. Issuers are trusted entities, such as governments, financial institutions, or employers, that create and digitally sign verifiable credentials. Holders (users) store these credentials in secure digital wallets, retaining full control over their identity information. Verifiers request proof of identity from users and validate cryptographic signatures to confirm authenticity without needing to contact the original issuer directly.

The core principle of SSI is decentralized identifiers (DIDs), which serve as globally unique, cryptographically verifiable identity records stored on blockchain networks or other decentralized ledgers. Unlike traditional identifiers (such as usernames, email addresses, or government-issued IDs), DIDs are self-generated by users and can be resolved through blockchain-based DID registries. Each DID is associated with a public-private key pair, allowing users to sign digital transactions and prove their identity without revealing unnecessary personal information.

Verifiable credentials (VCs) are the digital equivalents of physical identity documents, such as passports, driver's licenses, or employee badges, issued in an SSI ecosystem. These credentials contain claims about an identity, cryptographically signed by the issuer, ensuring authenticity and preventing forgery. When a verifier requests identity verification, the user can present a zero-knowledge proof (ZKP), demonstrating possession of valid credentials without disclosing sensitive details. ZKPs enhance privacy by allowing users to prove attributes (such as age or citizenship) without revealing the underlying credential details.

Blockchain plays a crucial role in ensuring trust in distributed identity verification systems by acting as a decentralized trust anchor. Rather than storing personal identity information directly on-chain, blockchain networks record DID documents, credential revocation registries, and cryptographic proofs that verifiers can reference to validate identity claims. Public blockchains such as Ethereum, Hyperledger Indy, and Sovrin support decentralized identity frameworks by enabling tamper-proof credential issuance, identity attestation, and revocation mechanisms.

One of the main benefits of blockchain-based SSI systems is eliminating identity silos and reducing dependency on centralized identity providers. Traditional identity models require users to maintain multiple accounts across different platforms, leading to password fatigue, account recovery challenges, and increased attack surfaces for identity theft. In contrast, a single decentralized identity can be used across multiple applications, ensuring seamless authentication, cross-domain trust, and enhanced security.

Interoperability is a key challenge in decentralized identity verification. SSI solutions must adhere to global identity standards, such as W3C Decentralized Identifiers (DIDs), Verifiable Credentials (VCs), and the DIF (Decentralized Identity Foundation) standards. By adopting interoperable identity schemas, SSI systems enable cross-border identity verification, allowing users to prove their identity across different organizations, industries, and jurisdictions without requiring redundant verification processes.

Enterprises integrating blockchain-based identity verification must implement secure digital wallets for managing decentralized identities and verifiable credentials. Wallet applications must support secure key storage, biometric authentication, hardware-backed encryption, and multi-device credential synchronization. Wallets can be implemented as mobile applications, browser extensions, or hardware-based security devices that allow users to manage their identities securely and present verifiable credentials when needed.

Privacy-preserving identity verification is another critical aspect of SSI. Traditional identity verification often requires sharing excessive amounts of personal data, increasing the risk of data breaches, identity theft, and privacy violations. With selective disclosure and zero-knowledge proofs, blockchain-based SSI systems minimize data exposure, allowing users to share only the necessary identity attributes for a specific transaction. For example, a user proving their eligibility for an age-restricted service can present proof that they are above the required age without disclosing their full birthdate.

Regulatory compliance plays a significant role in the adoption of decentralized identity verification systems. SSI implementations must align with data protection laws such as GDPR, CCPA, and NIST identity standards, ensuring that users have control over their personal data while maintaining compliance with legal identity verification requirements. Regulatory-compliant identity frameworks must support auditable credential issuance, consent-based data sharing, and real-time revocation mechanisms to prevent fraudulent or unauthorized identity claims.

Security threats in decentralized identity verification systems include private key compromise, Sybil attacks, identity fraud, and blockchain scalability limitations. To mitigate these risks, multi-factor authentication (MFA), hardware security modules (HSMs), and cryptographic key recovery mechanisms must be implemented. Decentralized identity governance frameworks can also establish reputation-based identity attestation models, where multiple trusted entities collectively verify and vouch for a user's identity, reducing the risk of identity fraud.

Blockchain-based SSI adoption continues to grow in financial services, healthcare, education, and government identity programs. Decentralized identity solutions enable digital banking with secure KYC (Know Your Customer) verification, protect patient records with blockchain-based health credentials, facilitate digital diplomas for educational institutions, and support self-sovereign e-government identity initiatives. These applications demonstrate the potential of trustless, secure, and user-controlled identity verification in a wide range of real-world scenarios.

Enterprises developing distributed identity verification systems must prioritize scalability, interoperability, and user experience to drive mainstream adoption. Hybrid blockchain architectures, where SSI credential issuance occurs on permissioned blockchains while verifications reference public blockchain trust anchors, provide an optimal balance between security, privacy, and performance. Decentralized identity bridges connecting SSI ecosystems with existing IAM platforms further accelerate enterprise integration, allowing businesses to adopt decentralized authentication alongside traditional IAM models.

By leveraging blockchain and Self-Sovereign Identity (SSI), organizations can build secure, privacy-enhancing, and user-controlled identity verification systems that eliminate reliance on centralized authorities, enhance interoperability across ecosystems, and protect digital identities against fraud and misuse.

Mitigating Insider Threats using IAM Anomaly Detection and UEBA

Insider threats pose a significant risk to enterprise security, as they originate from trusted users with legitimate access to systems, data, and applications. Unlike external attackers who must breach defenses, insiders already have privileged credentials and can misuse them for unauthorized activities, data exfiltration, or privilege escalation. Traditional security models based on role-based access control (RBAC) and static policies struggle to detect sophisticated insider threats, as these attacks often bypass perimeter defenses and occur over extended periods. To address this challenge, Identity and Access Management (IAM) anomaly detection and User and Entity Behavior Analytics (UEBA) provide advanced threat detection capabilities by continuously analyzing access patterns, monitoring deviations from normal behavior, and detecting suspicious activity in real-time.

IAM anomaly detection focuses on identifying deviations from expected access behavior, using machine learning and statistical models to assess risk dynamically. Traditional IAM systems enforce access policies based on predefined roles and permissions, but these policies often fail to adapt to contextual risk factors such as device type, geolocation, login frequency, and resource access behavior. By integrating anomaly detection models, IAM solutions can distinguish between legitimate and suspicious activities, reducing false positives while enhancing insider threat mitigation.

UEBA extends anomaly detection by analyzing user behavior over time, correlating authentication events, access requests, and privilege modifications to identify high-risk patterns. Unlike rule-based detection, which relies on predefined alerts, UEBA models dynamically learn user behavior baselines and detect outliers that indicate potential threats. For example, if an employee who typically accesses internal sales data suddenly attempts to download large volumes of confidential financial reports, UEBA can flag this activity as anomalous and trigger an alert for investigation.

Real-time access monitoring is essential for detecting insider threats before they escalate. IAM solutions integrated with UEBA continuously track user session activity, failed login attempts, privilege escalations, and unauthorized file transfers. Behavioral risk scoring assigns risk levels to user actions based on historical trends, security policies, and known attack patterns. High-risk users may be required to undergo additional authentication steps, restricted from performing sensitive actions, or flagged for security review.

One of the primary techniques for insider threat mitigation is adaptive authentication, where access control dynamically adjusts based on user risk scores. If a UEBA system detects unusual login behavior, such as access from an unfamiliar IP address or untrusted device, it can trigger multi-factor authentication (MFA) enforcement, requiring additional identity verification. For example, a privileged user accessing restricted systems from an unusual country may be required to provide biometric verification or confirm their login via a trusted mobile device.

IAM anomaly detection also helps prevent privilege abuse, where insiders exploit excessive access rights to perform unauthorized actions. Role-based access control alone is insufficient to prevent privilege misuse, as users may accumulate permissions over time due to role creep. UEBA analyzes historical access data, identifying privilege anomalies such as sudden escalations in user permissions, changes to access control lists (ACLs), and unauthorized role assignments. Security teams can use this data to enforce Just-In-Time (JIT) access, where privileges are granted only when needed and automatically revoked after the task is completed.

Detecting data exfiltration is a critical use case for IAM anomaly detection. Insiders attempting to steal sensitive information often exhibit behavioral indicators, such as exporting excessive files, accessing systems outside working hours, or modifying data classification labels. UEBA models correlate IAM logs with file access activity, detecting patterns indicative of potential data theft. Integration with Data Loss Prevention (DLP) solutions enables security teams to automatically block unauthorized file transfers, disable access to external storage devices, or encrypt sensitive files in real time.

For organizations operating in cloud environments, insider threats extend beyond traditional IAM controls. Cloud IAM solutions such as AWS IAM, Microsoft Entra ID (formerly Azure AD), and Google Cloud

IAM require continuous monitoring to detect misconfigured policies, unauthorized role assumptions, and suspicious API activity. UEBA for cloud IAM environments analyzes identity federation logs, cloud access patterns, and administrative actions to identify compromised credentials, insider privilege abuse, and unauthorized resource provisioning.

Integrating IAM anomaly detection with Security Information and Event Management (SIEM) platforms enhances real-time threat detection and forensic analysis. SIEM solutions such as Splunk, Elastic Security, and Microsoft Sentinel aggregate IAM logs, authentication records, and UEBA alerts, enabling security teams to correlate identity events with other security indicators. For example, if an insider threat actor attempts to disable audit logs or modify IAM policies, a SIEM-integrated IAM anomaly detection system can automatically trigger an incident response workflow.

Preventing insider account compromise requires continuous identity verification and session monitoring. Attackers often target privileged accounts through credential theft, phishing, and session hijacking. IAM anomaly detection can detect suspicious session behaviors, such as simultaneous logins from different geographic locations, credential reuse across multiple services, and anomalous session token lifetimes. Security teams can implement session revocation policies, where high-risk sessions are automatically terminated and require reauthentication.

UEBA models must be continuously trained on new identity threats, leveraging threat intelligence feeds, historical attack data, and machine learning updates to improve detection accuracy. Security teams should implement behavioral baselining strategies, where UEBA dynamically learns new user behaviors while filtering out benign deviations to reduce false positives. By integrating automated remediation mechanisms, IAM systems can suspend compromised accounts, revoke high-risk permissions, or trigger real-time incident response actions without human intervention.

For compliance-driven organizations, IAM anomaly detection and UEBA play a crucial role in meeting regulatory requirements such as GDPR, HIPAA, PCI-DSS, and NIST 800-53. Many security frameworks require continuous identity monitoring, access review automation, and least-privilege enforcement to mitigate insider threats. IAM anomaly detection solutions generate compliance reports, track access anomalies, and provide audit trails to support security governance and risk management initiatives.

By leveraging IAM anomaly detection and UEBA, enterprises can proactively identify and mitigate insider threats, enforcing dynamic access controls, detecting data exfiltration attempts, preventing privilege misuse, and ensuring regulatory compliance. Advanced identity threat detection technologies provide real-time visibility into user behavior, reducing the risk of insider-driven security incidents and strengthening overall IAM security posture.

IAM Compliance as Code: Automating Audits using Regula, OPA, and OpenSCAP

Identity and Access Management (IAM) compliance is a critical requirement for organizations operating in regulated industries, ensuring that security policies, access controls, and identity governance meet legal and industry standards. Traditional IAM audits rely on manual reviews, static compliance reports, and periodic assessments, which often fail to provide real-time visibility into security posture. To address this challenge, Compliance as Code (CaC) introduces a declarative, automated approach to IAM compliance, enabling organizations to define, enforce, and monitor security policies programmatically. By leveraging Regula, Open Policy Agent (OPA), and OpenSCAP, enterprises can continuously evaluate IAM configurations, detect policy violations, and ensure adherence to security frameworks such as NIST 800-53, GDPR, HIPAA, PCI-DSS, and ISO 27001.

Compliance as Code treats IAM security controls as machine-readable policies, allowing organizations to automate compliance checks across cloud environments, IAM systems, and infrastructure components. Instead of relying on spreadsheet-based audits and manual security reviews, IAM policies are written as code, version-controlled, and evaluated against real-time identity configurations. This approach ensures that non-compliant IAM configurations are detected immediately, reducing the risk of misconfigurations, excessive permissions, and access control failures.

Regula is an open-source tool designed for automated IAM policy validation and cloud compliance checks. It enables security teams to define compliance policies as code using Rego, the policy language of OPA, and apply them to AWS IAM, Azure AD, and Google Cloud IAM configurations. Regula scans IAM configurations to identify excessive privileges, misconfigured roles, weak password policies, and non-compliant authentication settings. For example, an IAM compliance policy in Regula can enforce that all IAM users must have multi-factor authentication (MFA) enabled, rejecting any configurations that do not meet this requirement.

Regula integrates seamlessly with CI/CD pipelines, allowing organizations to enforce IAM compliance at every stage of the development and deployment lifecycle. Before provisioning new IAM roles, policies, or service accounts, Regula evaluates security configurations against predefined compliance rules, ensuring that only compliant IAM configurations are deployed. This shift-left security approach prevents security misconfigurations from reaching production environments, reducing the risk of privilege escalation, unauthorized access, and credential leaks.

Open Policy Agent (OPA) extends IAM compliance automation by providing a flexible policy engine for defining and enforcing access control policies. OPA enables fine-grained IAM governance, evaluating access requests in real-time based on predefined compliance rules. By integrating OPA with IAM systems, organizations can enforce attribute-based access control (ABAC) policies, ensuring that users only receive permissions aligned with security policies. For example, an OPA policy can enforce that only employees with a security clearance level of "Confidential" can access sensitive cloud resources, dynamically granting or denying access based on real-time identity attributes.

OPA's policy decision engine is widely used in cloud-native IAM implementations, where microservices, Kubernetes clusters, and API gateways require dynamic access control. By embedding OPA into IAM authorization workflows, organizations can define security policies programmatically, preventing unauthorized access based on predefined compliance rules. OPA's RESTful API interface allows it to integrate with AWS IAM, Kubernetes RBAC, HashiCorp Vault, and OpenID Connect (OIDC)-based authentication providers, ensuring consistent access control enforcement across diverse IAM ecosystems.

OpenSCAP is a security automation and compliance auditing framework that provides predefined security benchmarks, vulnerability scanning, and compliance validation for IAM configurations. OpenSCAP supports CIS benchmarks, DISA STIGs, and NIST 800-53 security controls, allowing organizations to audit IAM policies, identity governance workflows, and authentication mechanisms against industry standards. OpenSCAP's automated compliance scanning ensures that IAM configurations remain compliant with regulatory frameworks, reducing the risk of access control violations and security misconfigurations.

One of the key advantages of Compliance as Code is continuous compliance monitoring, where IAM configurations are evaluated in real time rather than during scheduled audits. Instead of conducting periodic IAM security assessments, compliance policies are continuously enforced using automated scanning tools and policy-as-code frameworks. This approach ensures that security teams receive instant alerts when IAM configurations drift from compliance standards, allowing for immediate remediation.

IAM Compliance as Code also enhances auditability and traceability by maintaining a version-controlled history of IAM policy changes. Compliance policies are stored in Git repositories, enabling organizations to track policy modifications, enforcement decisions, and historical compliance states. This audit trail ensures regulatory transparency, allowing organizations to demonstrate compliance during security audits and forensic investigations.

Automating IAM compliance checks with Regula, OPA, and OpenSCAP reduces the reliance on manual security reviews, minimizing human errors and increasing the efficiency of compliance processes. Security teams no longer need to manually inspect IAM roles, permission assignments, and access policies, as policy-as-code frameworks automate these checks at scale. This automation ensures that IAM security policies remain consistent, repeatable, and aligned with industry best practices.

IAM compliance automation also plays a critical role in incident response and remediation. When a non-compliant IAM configuration is detected, policy enforcement tools can automatically trigger corrective actions, such as revoking excessive permissions, rotating compromised credentials, or disabling unauthorized IAM accounts. This proactive remediation approach prevents privileged access abuse, insider threats, and unauthorized identity modifications, strengthening IAM security posture.

For organizations operating in multi-cloud environments, Compliance as Code provides cross-platform IAM policy enforcement, ensuring consistent identity security across AWS, Azure, Google Cloud, and on-premises IAM systems. By defining IAM policies as vendor-agnostic compliance rules, organizations eliminate IAM security gaps caused by cloud misconfigurations, excessive privileges, and inconsistent identity governance policies.

Integrating machine learning-driven anomaly detection into Compliance as Code further enhances IAM security. By analyzing IAM access patterns, AI-driven compliance tools can detect deviations from normal behavior, identifying compromised accounts, privilege escalation attempts, and policy misconfigurations before they result in security breaches. Combining IAM anomaly detection with Compliance as Code ensures that access control decisions are continuously validated against evolving security threats.

By adopting Regula, OPA, and OpenSCAP, enterprises can automate IAM compliance checks, enforce security policies as code, and continuously monitor identity governance risks. This approach ensures that IAM security remains proactive, scalable, and adaptable, reducing compliance drift and enhancing regulatory adherence across enterprise IAM ecosystems.

IAM Incident Response Automation using SOAR (Security Orchestration, Automation, and Response)

Identity and Access Management (IAM) is a critical security layer that ensures users, applications, and devices authenticate and access resources securely. However, IAM systems are frequent targets of cyberattacks, including credential compromise, privilege escalation, insider threats, and identity fraud. Traditional incident response processes rely on manual security investigations, log analysis, and remediation actions, which are often slow and prone to human error. To mitigate identity-related threats efficiently, organizations are integrating Security Orchestration, Automation, and Response (SOAR) solutions into their IAM ecosystems. SOAR automates IAM incident response by orchestrating security workflows, enabling real-time threat detection, and executing predefined remediation actions without manual intervention.

SOAR platforms enhance IAM security by aggregating identity logs, authentication events, and access anomalies from multiple sources, including SIEM (Security Information and Event Management) platforms, IAM logs, cloud identity providers, and endpoint security solutions. These platforms analyze IAM-related alerts in real-time, applying automated playbooks to respond to suspicious identity activities. When an anomalous event, such as an unauthorized login attempt, suspicious role escalation, or unusual API access, is detected, SOAR can immediately initiate an automated response, reducing the risk of compromise.

IAM incidents often involve account takeovers, where attackers steal credentials and attempt to access privileged systems. Traditional security teams manually investigate these incidents by analyzing login attempts, reviewing identity logs, and verifying account activities. SOAR eliminates these manual processes by automating credential compromise detection. When an IAM system detects multiple failed login attempts, abnormal geolocation logins, or credential stuffing attacks, SOAR automatically triggers an account lockout, forces a password reset, or enforces multi-factor authentication (MFA) revalidation. These automated responses prevent attackers from exploiting compromised credentials while minimizing user disruption.

Privileged access abuse is another major IAM security risk. Attackers often target privileged accounts, service accounts, and administrative users to escalate access and perform unauthorized actions. SOAR integrates with Privileged Access Management (PAM) solutions, continuously monitoring privileged account activity and detecting unusual access patterns. If SOAR identifies unexpected privilege escalations, unauthorized privilege modifications, or excessive API token usage, it can automatically revoke elevated permissions, disable high-risk accounts, and alert security teams for further investigation.

IAM policy misconfigurations are a common cause of security breaches, leading to overly permissive access controls, misconfigured identity federation settings, and weak authentication policies. Manually identifying and correcting IAM misconfigurations across multi-cloud and hybrid environments is time-consuming and complex. SOAR automates IAM security policy enforcement by continuously auditing IAM roles, access permissions, and authentication rules against compliance frameworks such as NIST 800-53, CIS Benchmarks, and PCI-DSS. If a misconfiguration is detected, SOAR can automatically modify access policies, enforce least privilege principles, or revoke excessive permissions to mitigate risk.

Security teams often struggle with identity-related incident triage, as IAM logs generate a high volume of authentication events, failed logins, and access requests. Without automation, security analysts must manually correlate identity anomalies across multiple systems, leading to delayed responses and undetected threats. SOAR integrates threat intelligence feeds, anomaly detection algorithms, and behavioral analytics to enrich IAM incident data, prioritizing alerts based on risk scores and automating incident investigation workflows. When SOAR identifies a high-risk IAM incident, it can dynamically escalate the alert, notify security teams, and generate an incident report with enriched identity context.

Automating IAM forensic investigations is another critical capability of SOAR. When an identity-related breach occurs, security teams need to quickly trace the attack path, identify compromised accounts, and assess the impact of unauthorized access. SOAR enables automated forensic log analysis, correlating IAM audit trails, authentication records, and privilege changes across the environment. Security teams can use SOAR to generate a timeline of suspicious identity activities, identify lateral movement attempts, and determine whether sensitive data was accessed or exfiltrated.

SOAR also strengthens Zero Trust IAM architectures by enforcing continuous authentication and real-time risk assessment. Traditional IAM models rely on static authentication controls, where users authenticate once and retain access for extended sessions. This approach is vulnerable to session hijacking, token theft, and identity impersonation. SOAR enhances IAM security by integrating with risk-based authentication solutions, dynamically adjusting access privileges based on user behavior, device reputation, and geolocation. If SOAR detects a high-risk session, anomalous device fingerprinting, or identity spoofing attempts, it can enforce adaptive authentication policies, require step-up verification, or terminate suspicious sessions.

Security operations teams often face challenges in IAM incident response collaboration, as identity security incidents require coordination between IT administrators, security analysts, compliance teams, and IAM engineers. SOAR provides centralized incident response orchestration, enabling security teams to define IAM-specific playbooks that standardize response actions for common identity threats. These playbooks ensure consistent and repeatable incident handling, reducing dependency on manual decision-making and accelerating response times.

SOAR also enhances IAM compliance automation, ensuring organizations meet regulatory requirements by automating identity audit processes, access reviews, and identity governance enforcement. For example, SOAR can automate quarterly access certification campaigns, revoke inactive user accounts, and generate compliance reports to support audits. By integrating with IAM governance tools such as SailPoint, Okta, and Microsoft Entra ID, SOAR ensures that IAM security controls align with compliance mandates, reducing the risk of regulatory violations.

Multi-cloud IAM environments introduce additional complexity, as organizations must manage IAM security across AWS, Azure, Google Cloud, and on-premises identity platforms. SOAR integrates with cloud-native IAM services, enabling automated cross-cloud IAM security monitoring, misconfiguration detection, and access policy enforcement. If SOAR detects unauthorized cross-cloud access attempts, role misconfigurations, or high-risk API token usage, it can initiate automated incident response workflows, enforce cloud IAM security policies, and trigger real-time remediations.

For security teams adopting AI-driven threat detection, SOAR can integrate with machine learning-powered IAM analytics platforms, enabling automated identity risk prediction, anomaly detection, and user behavior scoring. AI-enhanced SOAR solutions analyze historical identity threats, correlate IAM security incidents, and proactively recommend risk mitigation strategies. These capabilities help organizations predict identity threats before they escalate, allowing security teams to take preemptive action against high-risk IAM activities.

By leveraging SOAR for IAM incident response automation, organizations can reduce manual security workloads, accelerate incident detection and remediation, enforce adaptive identity security controls, and improve compliance posture. Automated IAM incident response ensures proactive identity threat mitigation, minimizes security gaps, and enhances overall enterprise security resilience.

Developing Custom OAuth2 Grant Types for Enterprise Applications

OAuth 2.0 is the de facto standard for authorization in modern enterprise applications, enabling secure and scalable access to protected resources across cloud, mobile, and web applications. While OAuth 2.0 defines several standard grant types, including Authorization Code, Client Credentials, Resource Owner Password Credentials (ROPC), and Device Code, enterprises often have unique security, compliance, and integration requirements that necessitate custom OAuth2 grant types. Developing custom grant types allows organizations to extend OAuth 2.0 workflows to accommodate specialized authentication mechanisms, federated identity models, and advanced security controls.

Custom OAuth2 grant types are implemented by modifying the OAuth authorization server to support new token exchange workflows that meet business-specific needs. These grant types define how clients authenticate, request tokens, and obtain access to protected resources, incorporating custom identity validation, multi-factor authentication (MFA) enforcement, or risk-based access control policies. Unlike standard grant types, which follow predefined OAuth flows, custom grant types allow custom business logic to be embedded within the authorization process, ensuring that enterprise security and compliance requirements are met.

One of the primary reasons for developing custom OAuth2 grant types is integrating with non-standard authentication mechanisms, such as legacy identity providers, hardware security modules (HSMs), biometric authentication, and blockchain-based identity verification. Many enterprises maintain legacy authentication systems that do not support modern OAuth2 flows. A custom grant type can act as a bridge between legacy authentication workflows and OAuth-based access management, allowing enterprises to modernize security architectures without disrupting existing authentication infrastructures.

A key consideration when designing custom grant types is defining how access tokens are issued and validated. Standard OAuth2 grant types rely on well-defined flows, but a custom grant type may introduce additional authentication steps, external validation services, or conditional token issuance rules. For example, an enterprise requiring adaptive authentication based on user risk scores can develop a custom grant type that dynamically evaluates risk attributes before issuing an access token. If a login attempt is deemed high-risk, the custom grant type can enforce step-up authentication before granting access.

Custom OAuth2 grant types can also enhance federated authentication workflows by incorporating external identity providers, security assertion validation, and dynamic policy enforcement. For instance, an enterprise integrating multiple federated identity providers (IdPs) may develop a custom grant type that dynamically selects the appropriate

IdP based on user attributes. Instead of requiring separate OAuth flows for each IdP, the custom grant type centralizes federated authentication logic, streamlining user experience and security management.

Security is a critical aspect of custom OAuth2 grant type development, requiring robust token lifecycle management, secure token storage, and dynamic access control policies. Custom grant types must adhere to OAuth2 security best practices, including token expiration, refresh token rotation, audience restriction, and cryptographic token signing. Enterprises should implement JSON Web Token (JWT)-based access tokens with asymmetric key signing (RS256, ES256) to prevent token forgery. Additionally, OAuth introspection endpoints should be utilized to validate active tokens, ensuring that compromised or revoked tokens are immediately invalidated.

Developing a custom OAuth2 grant type involves extending the authorization server's token endpoint to support additional grant processing logic. Most OAuth2 servers, including Keycloak, ForgeRock AM, Okta, and Autho, provide custom extension points that allow developers to define new grant types. For example, in Keycloak, custom grant types can be implemented using Java-based authentication flows, enabling organizations to inject external authentication factors, enforce dynamic access control, and integrate with risk engines. Similarly, ForgeRock AM supports custom authentication modules that modify token issuance policies, allowing enterprises to enforce policy-driven access decisions based on real-time identity attributes.

A practical example of a custom OAuth2 grant type is a Hardware Security Token (HST) Grant, designed for enterprises requiring hardware-backed authentication before issuing access tokens. In this grant type, a user authenticates using a FIDO2/WebAuthn security key, and the authorization server verifies the cryptographic proof before issuing an OAuth2 access token. This workflow enhances security by binding authentication to a physical device, preventing credential theft and unauthorized access.

Another example is a Delegated Identity Validation Grant, where a trusted third-party service acts as an identity validator before issuing OAuth tokens. In this scenario, an enterprise integrating external identity proofing services (such as KYC providers, government ID verification, or biometric authentication platforms) can use a custom grant type to validate a user's identity before granting access to protected resources. This is especially useful for regulated industries requiring identity verification before issuing authentication credentials.

A critical challenge in implementing custom OAuth2 grant types is ensuring backward compatibility and interoperability with existing OAuth2 clients and API gateways. Enterprises must provide comprehensive developer documentation, SDKs, and example implementations to facilitate adoption of the custom grant type. Additionally, OAuth2 client libraries should be extended to support the new grant type, ensuring that existing applications can integrate with the custom authentication workflow seamlessly.

Logging and monitoring are essential components of custom OAuth2 grant type implementations. Enterprises should integrate real-time logging and security analytics to track token issuance, access attempts, and anomalous authentication patterns. OAuth logs should be ingested into SIEM (Security Information and Event Management) platforms, enabling threat detection, compliance auditing, and incident response. Additionally, security teams should implement automated token revocation mechanisms to detect and mitigate compromised OAuth tokens.

Integrating OAuth 2.0 Demonstration of Proof-of-Possession (DPoP) into custom grant types enhances security by ensuring that access tokens are bound to the original client that requested them. Unlike standard OAuth bearer tokens, which can be stolen and reused, DPoP tokens require cryptographic proof of possession, preventing token replay attacks. Enterprises implementing high-security OAuth2 workflows should consider using DPoP for sensitive API transactions, ensuring that OAuth tokens cannot be misused by unauthorized clients.

Custom OAuth2 grant types also play a role in zero-trust identity architectures, enabling adaptive authentication, risk-aware access control, and continuous verification. By integrating machine learning-driven identity risk scoring, custom grant types can dynamically adjust authentication requirements based on user behavior, device reputation, and historical access trends. This ensures that authentication policies evolve in response to emerging threats, reducing the risk of account takeovers, privilege escalation, and identity fraud.

By developing custom OAuth2 grant types, enterprises can extend standard OAuth workflows to meet complex security, compliance, and integration requirements, ensuring scalable and secure identity management across modern applications. Custom grants enable organizations to tailor authentication and authorization policies while enhancing security, enabling adaptive access control, and integrating with advanced identity verification mechanisms.

Integrating IAM with SIEM Solutions (Splunk, ELK, Azure Sentinel) for Advanced Threat Hunting

Identity and Access Management (IAM) is a critical component of enterprise security, ensuring that users, applications, and devices are authenticated and authorized securely. However, IAM systems alone do not provide full visibility into identity-based threats, privilege escalations, or anomalous access patterns. To enhance security operations, organizations integrate IAM solutions with Security Information and Event Management (SIEM) platforms such as Splunk, ELK (Elasticsearch, Logstash, Kibana), and Azure Sentinel. This integration enables real-time threat detection, forensic investigations, and automated response actions, significantly improving an enterprise's ability to detect, analyze, and mitigate identity-based threats.

SIEM platforms aggregate, normalize, and correlate security logs from multiple sources, including IAM platforms, authentication logs, privileged access management (PAM) systems, endpoint security tools, and network firewalls. By centralizing identity-related logs, security teams gain comprehensive visibility into authentication events, access policy changes, failed login attempts, and privilege escalations. Advanced threat hunting techniques leverage machine learning-driven anomaly detection, behavioral analytics, and threat intelligence feeds to identify malicious activities within IAM environments.

A successful IAM-SIEM integration requires configuring IAM systems to send authentication, authorization, and access control logs to the SIEM platform. Most IAM solutions, such as Microsoft Entra ID (formerly Azure AD), Okta, Ping Identity, and AWS IAM, provide event streaming, log forwarding, and API-based SIEM integration. Syslog, JSON, and Common Event Format (CEF) are commonly used log formats for ensuring structured and machine-readable event ingestion into SIEM platforms.

Splunk is a widely used SIEM solution that provides powerful log ingestion, correlation, and search capabilities for IAM data. By integrating IAM logs into Splunk Enterprise Security (ES), security teams can build real-time dashboards, create identity threat detection rules, and automate remediation actions. Splunk's Search Processing Language (SPL) enables organizations to detect brute-force attacks, identify privilege escalation attempts, and correlate IAM activities with network threats. For example, a Splunk correlation rule can flag a user attempting to log in from multiple geographic locations within a short time frame, indicating possible session hijacking or credential compromise.

The ELK stack (Elasticsearch, Logstash, Kibana) provides open-source SIEM capabilities for ingesting, analyzing, and visualizing IAM security logs. Logstash collects IAM logs, Elasticsearch indexes the data, and Kibana provides interactive visualizations for threat analysis. Security teams can build custom IAM dashboards in Kibana that display failed authentication trends, anomalous access patterns, and real-time IAM policy violations. Elasticsearch Query Language (EQL) allows security analysts to search for identity threats, detect suspicious login attempts, and analyze privilege changes. By leveraging machine learning models within ELK, organizations can detect deviations from normal IAM behavior, such as unexpected access to high-risk resources or administrative privilege modifications.

Azure Sentinel, Microsoft's cloud-native SIEM and SOAR (Security Orchestration, Automation, and Response) platform, provides deep IAM integration with Microsoft Entra ID, Azure AD Conditional Access policies, and Microsoft Defender for Identity. Sentinel ingests IAM logs via Azure Monitor, Log Analytics, and Event Hubs, allowing security teams to detect identity-based threats in cloud and hybrid environments. Sentinel's Kusto Query Language (KQL) enables advanced identity analytics, allowing analysts to identify compromised accounts, detect insider threats, and track anomalous sign-in behavior. Sentinel also integrates with Microsoft's Threat Intelligence, enriching IAM threat detection with global attack patterns and known adversary tactics.

IAM integration with SIEM enables real-time detection of identity-based attacks, including credential stuffing, password spraying, and privilege escalation exploits. Attackers frequently target IAM misconfigurations, weak authentication policies, and excessive privileges to gain unauthorized access. SIEM correlation rules help identify unauthorized access attempts, detect service account abuse, and flag anomalies in role assignments. Security teams can define threshold-based alerts, where excessive failed login attempts within a short timeframe trigger automatic account lockdowns, MFA revalidation, or temporary session suspensions.

Threat hunting using IAM logs involves proactively searching for indicators of compromise (IoCs), suspicious identity behavior, and lateral movement patterns. SIEM threat hunters use query-based detection techniques, machine learning-based anomaly scoring, and behavioral baselining to uncover stealthy adversary techniques that evade standard security controls. For example, IAM-SIEM correlation rules can detect when an attacker gains access to a low-privilege account, escalates permissions, and exfiltrates sensitive data before executing a ransomware attack or supply chain compromise.

SIEM platforms also enable privileged access monitoring, ensuring that high-risk administrative actions are continuously logged and analyzed. Security teams can configure privileged user behavior analytics (PUBA) to detect unexpected role modifications, suspicious API key usage, and unauthorized access to sensitive IAM configurations. For example, if a privileged administrator disables security logging, modifies IAM audit policies, or adds an unauthorized user to a critical access group, SIEM alerts can immediately trigger security workflows, revoke unauthorized changes, and notify incident response teams.

IAM-SIEM integration enhances Zero Trust security architectures, ensuring that every access request is continuously monitored, analyzed, and dynamically assessed for risk. Security teams can enforce adaptive IAM controls based on real-time SIEM alerts, such as blocking access for users exhibiting high-risk behavior, enforcing step-up authentication for sensitive operations, or triggering identity verification workflows when anomalies are detected.

Automated SOAR (Security Orchestration, Automation, and Response) workflows extend IAM-SIEM integration by automatically responding to identity-related incidents. When a SIEM detects a compromised IAM account, an unusual login attempt, or a privilege escalation event, SOAR can execute predefined playbooks that automatically revoke access, disable suspicious accounts, and trigger IAM access reviews. For example, an automated SOAR workflow can terminate all active sessions for a high-risk user, generate an incident report, and require the user to reauthenticate using MFA before regaining access.

IAM compliance auditing also benefits from SIEM integration by ensuring that access control policies align with regulatory requirements such as GDPR, HIPAA, NIST 800-53, and PCI-DSS. SIEM platforms generate real-time IAM compliance reports, track IAM security violations, and provide forensic audit trails for regulatory inspections. Security teams can schedule automated IAM policy audits, ensuring that access reviews, role changes, and authentication policies remain compliant with industry standards.

Integrating IAM with SIEM solutions like Splunk, ELK, and Azure Sentinel transforms identity security into a real-time, analytics-driven process, allowing security teams to detect, investigate, and respond to identity threats with greater speed and accuracy. By leveraging advanced threat hunting, automated response workflows, and adaptive security policies, organizations strengthen IAM defenses and proactively mitigate identity-based cyber threats.

IAM Identity Graph Modeling: Graph Databases for Identity Relationship Management

Identity and Access Management (IAM) is central to securing enterprise environments, ensuring that users, applications, and services have the appropriate access to resources. Traditional IAM systems rely on hierarchical directory structures and relational databases to store identity attributes, roles, and access policies. However, as organizations adopt zero-trust security models, dynamic access controls, and multi-cloud architectures, traditional approaches struggle to model complex identity relationships, role hierarchies, and cross-domain trust structures. Graph databases provide a more efficient, scalable, and flexible approach to identity relationship management by representing users, roles, permissions, and access entitlements as interconnected nodes and edges.

Graph-based IAM identity modeling enables organizations to visualize and analyze relationships between identities, access policies, privileges, and authentication events. Unlike traditional relational databases, which require complex joins and queries to retrieve related identity data, graph databases efficiently traverse identity relationships in real-time, making them ideal for IAM use cases that involve dynamic access control, privilege analysis, and attack path detection.

A graph-based IAM identity model consists of nodes (entities such as users, roles, groups, and resources) and edges (relationships between entities, such as role assignments, access rights, and authentication sessions). This structure allows organizations to map out identity relationships dynamically, ensuring that privilege inheritance, access policy enforcement, and identity governance remain continuously updated.

One of the most powerful use cases for IAM identity graph modeling is visualizing role-based access control (RBAC) and attribute-based access control (ABAC) relationships. In a traditional IAM system, roles and permissions are assigned in a flat or hierarchical structure, which can become unmanageable as organizations grow. A graph-based

RBAC model allows security teams to see how roles are inherited, how access propagates across different organizational units, and whether privilege escalation risks exist. By analyzing the graph structure of role assignments, organizations can identify role redundancies, detect overprivileged users, and optimize access policies dynamically.

In an ABAC implementation, graph databases store attribute relationships such as user location, department, device trust level, and security clearance as graph nodes, allowing real-time policy evaluation based on dynamic conditions. If a user requests access to a sensitive resource, the IAM system can quickly traverse the identity graph to determine whether the request complies with attribute-based security policies, ensuring that context-aware access decisions are enforced.

Graph IAM modeling is also instrumental in identity lifecycle management, where user onboarding, role transitions, and account deprovisioning must be tracked. Traditional IAM systems often struggle with stale access permissions and orphaned accounts, leading to privilege creep and security risks. A graph-based IAM system enables organizations to track identity lifecycle changes in real time, ensuring that users only retain permissions relevant to their current job role and responsibilities. If a user changes departments or leaves the organization, graph traversal queries can quickly identify and revoke unnecessary access rights across multiple systems.

Another critical use case for graph-based IAM modeling is privileged access management (PAM) and insider threat detection. Attackers often attempt to escalate privileges or move laterally within an organization's IAM system. Graph databases enable security teams to map out attack paths, detect suspicious privilege escalations, and uncover hidden relationships between privileged accounts. By continuously analyzing IAM graphs, security teams can detect privilege misuse, identify toxic role combinations, and implement automated risk-based access control policies.

Graph-based IAM models also enhance identity federation and cross-domain authentication by mapping trust relationships between multiple identity providers (IdPs), cloud IAM solutions, and enterprise authentication services. In a federated IAM environment, organizations must maintain trust mappings between external and internal identities while enforcing security policies consistently. A graph database allows security teams to visualize federated identity relationships, ensuring that trust chains are properly managed, and access policies remain enforced across distributed environments.

Threat intelligence and IAM security analytics benefit from graph-based anomaly detection and behavioral analysis. Graph databases enable user and entity behavior analytics (UEBA) by modeling identity activity patterns, such as logins, access requests, API calls, and privilege modifications, as graph nodes and edges. By applying graph-based machine learning algorithms, security teams can identify anomalous access patterns, detect compromised accounts, and prevent identity-based attacks before they escalate.

IAM compliance and auditability also improve with graph-based access control models. Security teams must regularly conduct access certification reviews, compliance audits, and security assessments to ensure that IAM policies align with regulatory standards such as GDPR, HIPAA, PCI-DSS, and NIST 800-53. Traditional IAM compliance audits require manual data aggregation and review, which is time-consuming and error-prone. By using graph-based IAM analytics, organizations can automate access reviews, generate real-time compliance reports, and track policy violations with precision.

Leading graph database technologies such as Neo4j, Amazon Neptune, and Microsoft Azure Cosmos DB provide native graph traversal and query capabilities optimized for IAM use cases. Security teams can leverage Cypher (Neo4j's query language) or Gremlin (Apache TinkerPop's graph query language) to perform complex identity relationship queries, detect security risks, and enforce dynamic access policies. For example, a Cypher query can identify all users with indirect access to a privileged system, detect nested role assignments, or find accounts exhibiting abnormal authentication behaviors.

Integrating IAM identity graphs with SIEM (Security Information and Event Management) and SOAR (Security Orchestration, Automation, and Response) platforms enhances real-time threat detection and automated incident response. By ingesting IAM graph data into SIEM solutions like Splunk, ELK, or Azure Sentinel, security teams can correlate identity events with other security logs, improving incident detection accuracy and forensic investigations. Additionally, SOAR workflows can use graph-based IAM threat intelligence to automatically revoke compromised credentials, escalate privilege alerts, and enforce risk-based access controls.

Organizations implementing zero-trust security architectures benefit significantly from IAM identity graph modeling. Zero-trust requires continuous verification, least-privilege access, and dynamic policy enforcement based on real-time identity attributes and behavioral insights. Graph-based IAM models allow organizations to visualize access relationships dynamically, prevent overprivileged access, and enforce zero-trust identity verification policies across the enterprise.

By adopting IAM identity graph modeling with graph databases, enterprises can enhance identity governance, strengthen access controls, improve security analytics, and enforce compliance automation. Graph-based identity models provide a scalable, real-time, and flexible approach to managing complex IAM ecosystems, ensuring that identity relationships remain secure, auditable, and optimized for modern security requirements.

Creating Serverless Identity Proofing and Risk-Based Authentication (RBA) Services

Identity proofing and risk-based authentication (RBA) are essential components of modern Identity and Access Management (IAM), ensuring that users are who they claim to be and adapting authentication requirements based on contextual risk. Traditional identity verification methods rely on static credentials and manual review processes, which are prone to fraud, inefficiencies, and scalability issues. By leveraging serverless architectures, organizations can build scalable, event-driven, and cost-effective identity proofing and RBA services that dynamically assess authentication risk and enforce adaptive security controls.

Serverless identity proofing enables organizations to verify user identities without maintaining dedicated authentication servers. Instead of relying on monolithic identity verification systems, cloud-based serverless functions orchestrate document verification, biometric validation, and external identity attestation in a distributed manner. Serverless platforms such as AWS Lambda, Azure Functions, and Google Cloud Functions process identity verification requests on demand, eliminating the need for persistent compute resources while providing near-instantaneous response times.

A typical serverless identity proofing workflow begins with a user submitting a government-issued ID, biometric scan, or digital signature to a verification service. The submitted information is then analyzed using AI-powered identity proofing services such as Amazon Rekognition, Microsoft Entra Verified ID, or Google Cloud Identity Verification. These services compare document authenticity, match facial biometrics, and check for fraud indicators. A serverless function coordinates the verification steps, validates the identity against trusted data sources, such as national identity registries or financial institutions, and generates a proof-of-identity token that downstream applications can trust.

Risk-based authentication (RBA) enhances IAM security by dynamically adjusting authentication requirements based on real-time risk assessments. Instead of applying static MFA policies to all users, RBA evaluates user behavior, device attributes, geolocation, network risk, and anomaly detection signals to determine whether additional verification is necessary. A serverless RBA engine operates by collecting risk telemetry from multiple identity sources, evaluating risk scores in real time, and enforcing adaptive authentication policies.

A serverless RBA service consists of multiple components, including event-driven authentication analysis, machine learning-based anomaly detection, and risk-aware policy enforcement. When a user attempts to authenticate, an AWS Lambda function or an Azure Function retrieves user context, historical access patterns, and device trust scores from a centralized risk database. The function calculates a risk score using statistical models, AI-powered behavioral analytics, and real-time threat intelligence feeds. If the risk score exceeds a predefined threshold, the system triggers step-up authentication, requiring additional verification such as biometric authentication, FIDO2 security keys, or one-time passcodes (OTPs).

Serverless architectures enable scalable, real-time risk-based authentication processing by leveraging cloud-native services such as AWS Step Functions, Azure Event Grid, and Google Cloud Pub/Sub. These services allow authentication events to be asynchronously processed, ensuring that risk evaluations do not introduce latency into authentication workflows. Additionally, serverless functions integrate with SIEM (Security Information and Event Management) platforms, feeding real-time risk insights into Splunk, ELK, or Azure Sentinel for advanced threat correlation and security analysis.

One of the key advantages of serverless identity proofing and RBA is fraud detection and prevention. Attackers frequently attempt credential stuffing, session hijacking, and identity spoofing to bypass authentication mechanisms. By continuously monitoring authentication anomalies, serverless RBA services detect suspicious login attempts, block high-risk authentication sessions, and alert security teams in real time. A common use case is detecting impossible travel scenarios, where a user attempts to log in from multiple locations within a short timeframe. Serverless RBA can automatically challenge these sessions with biometric authentication or deny access entirely based on risk policies.

Integrating machine learning models into serverless RBA services further enhances authentication security. AI-powered anomaly detection models, such as Amazon SageMaker, Azure Machine Learning, or Google Cloud AI Platform, continuously analyze historical login behavior, device fingerprints, and authentication success rates to generate adaptive risk scores. Serverless functions call these models during authentication events, enabling real-time AI-driven decision-making for access control.

Serverless identity proofing and RBA also enhance passwordless authentication strategies by ensuring that high-risk login attempts require stronger authentication mechanisms. Traditional IAM systems rely on static passwords, which are vulnerable to phishing, brute-force attacks, and credential leaks. A serverless RBA engine dynamically adjusts authentication strength, allowing passwordless logins with WebAuthn security keys for low-risk users while enforcing additional verification steps for high-risk scenarios.

Privacy and regulatory compliance are critical considerations in serverless identity proofing. Enterprises must ensure that identity verification data complies with GDPR, CCPA, and NIST 800-63 digital identity guidelines. Serverless architectures facilitate privacy-preserving identity proofing by leveraging edge processing, encryption-at-rest, and short-lived verification tokens. Instead of storing sensitive identity documents in centralized IAM databases, serverless functions process identity verification requests ephemerally, ensuring that user data is not retained beyond the verification session.

Serverless identity proofing also supports decentralized identity (DID) and verifiable credentials (VCs). Instead of relying on traditional identity providers, organizations can issue blockchain-backed identity proofs that allow users to control their own credentials. A serverless identity proofing function issues verifiable credentials using standards such as W3C DIDs and the Decentralized Identity Foundation (DIF). When a user attempts to authenticate, a serverless function verifies the cryptographic validity of the credential, checking blockchain registries for revocation status and fraud indicators.

To ensure scalability and cost optimization, serverless identity proofing and RBA services follow event-driven architectures, where functions execute only when triggered by authentication events. Unlike monolithic IAM systems that maintain persistent authentication servers, serverless functions operate on demand, reducing compute costs and optimizing resource allocation. Enterprises can further optimize cost by batch-processing authentication risk evaluations, using serverless data pipelines such as AWS Kinesis, Azure Data Factory, and Google Cloud Dataflow to aggregate identity risk telemetry efficiently.

A robust serverless identity proofing and RBA architecture integrates with existing IAM solutions, identity providers (IdPs), and authentication frameworks. Modern IAM platforms such as Okta, Ping Identity, and ForgeRock offer API-based integration with serverless authentication services, allowing organizations to extend existing authentication workflows with adaptive risk assessment and fraud detection. Serverless identity verification APIs provide secure authentication tokens that downstream IAM services can trust, ensuring frictionless and secure access across enterprise applications.

By leveraging serverless identity proofing and risk-based authentication, organizations achieve scalable, real-time identity verification, fraud-resistant authentication, and adaptive security enforcement. Serverless architectures reduce operational overhead, eliminate authentication bottlenecks, and provide a cost-effective approach to identity security, ensuring high-assurance authentication in an increasingly threat-driven digital landscape.

IAM Logging and Analytics using OpenTelemetry and Fluentd

Identity and Access Management (IAM) logging and analytics are essential for securing enterprise environments, detecting anomalous authentication events, and ensuring compliance with security frameworks. Traditional IAM logging mechanisms rely on centralized security logs from authentication providers, directory services, and access management platforms. However, as organizations adopt distributed architectures, microservices, and cloud-native IAM solutions, traditional logging approaches become insufficient. OpenTelemetry and Fluentd provide scalable, real-time, and structured IAM telemetry collection, enabling organizations to track authentication attempts, monitor access policies, and detect privilege escalation risks across cloud and on-premises environments.

IAM logs contain valuable security insights, including user authentication events, failed login attempts, role modifications, session activity, and access control violations. OpenTelemetry offers a standardized framework for collecting, instrumenting, and exporting IAM telemetry data, while Fluentd acts as a log aggregation and forwarding tool, ensuring that identity-related logs are structured, enriched, and routed to SIEM (Security Information and Event Management) platforms for analysis.

One of the main advantages of OpenTelemetry for IAM logging is its ability to instrument authentication workflows and access control decisions without modifying existing IAM implementations. OpenTelemetry provides language-agnostic SDKs and APIs that allow developers to capture IAM traces, metrics, and logs from identity providers, authentication servers, and authorization gateways. Unlike traditional logging frameworks that rely on log file parsing, OpenTelemetry enables event-driven IAM telemetry collection, allowing organizations to correlate real-time authentication signals with security threats and anomalous access patterns.

IAM telemetry instrumentation using OpenTelemetry involves attaching tracing spans to authentication events, such as user logins, token validations, role assignments, and MFA challenges. Each span records detailed metadata, including user identifiers, session tokens, access levels, and request timestamps, enabling security teams to reconstruct authentication event sequences for forensic investigations. OpenTelemetry propagates IAM trace context across microservices, ensuring that security teams can track identity transactions across distributed applications, cloud environments, and federated authentication domains.

Fluentd complements OpenTelemetry by aggregating and normalizing IAM logs, ensuring that identity-related telemetry is structured, parsed, and forwarded to centralized logging platforms. Fluentd uses input plugins to collect logs from multiple IAM sources, including LDAP servers, OAuth token issuers, OpenID Connect (OIDC) providers, and privileged access management (PAM) systems. Once collected, Fluentd enriches IAM logs with additional metadata, such as geolocation, device fingerprinting, and behavioral risk scores, allowing security teams to conduct context-aware identity threat analysis.

Fluentd's log routing capabilities enable organizations to stream IAM telemetry to multiple destinations, including SIEM platforms (Splunk, ELK, Azure Sentinel), security data lakes, and real-time analytics engines. Security teams can define custom Fluentd pipelines that filter, transform, and correlate IAM logs before forwarding them to security monitoring platforms. For example, Fluentd can be configured to extract failed authentication attempts, identify brute-force login patterns, and flag unauthorized role changes, ensuring that IAM-related security events receive priority in incident response workflows.

One of the key benefits of using OpenTelemetry for IAM analytics is real-time anomaly detection and risk-based access monitoring. By instrumenting IAM authentication flows with OpenTelemetry traces, security teams can build machine learning models that detect behavioral anomalies, privilege misuse, and unauthorized access patterns. OpenTelemetry's dynamic metric collection allows organizations to track IAM risk scores, failed authentication rates, and privilege escalation attempts, triggering automated response actions based on detected anomalies.

IAM compliance auditing requires detailed log retention, audit trails, and access review reports, ensuring that organizations meet security regulations such as GDPR, HIPAA, PCI-DSS, and NIST 800-53. Fluentd simplifies IAM compliance by normalizing authentication logs into structured formats (JSON, CEF, or Syslog), enabling auditors to query, filter, and analyze access records efficiently. Security teams can use Fluentd to generate IAM compliance dashboards, automate access reviews, and correlate identity governance violations with regulatory frameworks.

For cloud-native IAM architectures, OpenTelemetry and Fluentd provide scalable logging solutions that integrate with Kubernetes, AWS IAM, Azure Active Directory, and Google Cloud Identity. Fluentd's Kubernetes log collectors aggregate IAM telemetry from containerized identity services, ensuring that authentication logs from service meshes, API gateways, and federated authentication providers are centrally stored and analyzed. OpenTelemetry's Kubernetes instrumentation capabilities allow security teams to track IAM service dependencies, detect IAM-related Kubernetes misconfigurations, and analyze containerized access logs in real time.

IAM security monitoring benefits from Fluentd's log enrichment capabilities, where raw authentication logs are enhanced with external security intelligence feeds, known attacker IP databases, and threat correlation engines. By enriching IAM logs with contextual security data, organizations can detect credential stuffing attacks, identify compromised accounts, and prevent unauthorized API key usage. Fluentd's stream processing capabilities enable real-time identity anomaly detection, ensuring that high-risk authentication events trigger automated security responses, including session revocation, MFA enforcement, or IAM policy modifications.

Integrating OpenTelemetry and Fluentd with SIEM and SOAR (Security Orchestration, Automation, and Response) platforms enhances automated IAM incident detection and response. When IAM logs indicate suspicious authentication behavior, unauthorized privilege modifications, or API token abuse, security teams can leverage Fluentd's event forwarding to send high-priority IAM security alerts to SIEM platforms such as Splunk Enterprise Security, Elastic Security, or Microsoft Sentinel. SOAR platforms then execute automated response workflows, blocking malicious IAM activities and revoking compromised credentials.

IAM log analytics powered by OpenTelemetry and Fluentd also support threat hunting, where security analysts proactively search for identity-based attack patterns, unauthorized role escalations, and failed MFA attempts. Fluentd allows security teams to query historical IAM logs, detect long-term identity abuse trends, and correlate IAM anomalies with network and endpoint security telemetry. OpenTelemetry's distributed tracing capabilities provide deep visibility into IAM authentication workflows, ensuring that security teams can investigate identity-related incidents with precision.

Zero-trust IAM architectures rely on continuous authentication monitoring, dynamic risk-based access control, and real-time security analytics, all of which require scalable and structured IAM telemetry. OpenTelemetry and Fluentd enable zero-trust identity visibility, ensuring that every authentication attempt, privilege escalation event, and access control decision is continuously logged, analyzed, and correlated with security policies. By enforcing adaptive IAM security controls based on OpenTelemetry risk metrics, organizations strengthen their zero-trust identity governance framework.

By leveraging OpenTelemetry and Fluentd for IAM logging and analytics, organizations gain real-time identity visibility, advanced authentication monitoring, and automated threat detection capabilities. These tools enable scalable, cost-effective, and high-fidelity IAM telemetry processing, ensuring that identity-based security events are continuously monitored, analyzed, and acted upon in an increasingly complex threat landscape.

Developing High-Performance IAM Solutions for Millions of Identities

Identity and Access Management (IAM) solutions must be designed to handle authentication, authorization, and identity governance at scale. In modern enterprise environments, cloud platforms, and consumer-facing applications, IAM systems must support millions of identities, high-volume authentication requests, and dynamic access control policies while maintaining low latency, high availability, and strong security. Traditional monolithic IAM architectures struggle to scale efficiently under extreme load, leading to authentication bottlenecks, authorization delays, and performance degradation. To address these challenges, high-performance IAM solutions leverage distributed architectures, caching strategies, optimized data models, and event-driven processing to ensure seamless identity management at scale.

A core requirement for high-performance IAM solutions is horizontal scalability, ensuring that authentication and authorization services can handle millions of concurrent users. Cloud-native IAM architectures deploy microservices, containerized identity components, and serverless authentication functions to distribute identity workloads efficiently. Instead of relying on single-node directory services or relational databases, high-scale IAM solutions utilize distributed identity stores such as AWS DynamoDB, Google Cloud Spanner, or Apache Cassandra, which provide low-latency identity lookups and high availability across multiple data centers.

Authentication latency is a critical performance metric in large-scale IAM environments. Traditional authentication workflows, such as OAuth 2.0, OpenID Connect (OIDC), and SAML-based Single Sign-On (SSO), introduce overhead due to token issuance, validation, and cryptographic signature verification. To reduce authentication delays, high-performance IAM solutions implement JWT-based access tokens with asymmetric signing (RS256, ES256), token pre-validation mechanisms, and distributed session caches. By leveraging stateless authentication models, IAM systems eliminate the need for centralized session storage, significantly reducing authentication round-trip times.

High-scale IAM solutions also optimize directory services and identity repositories to ensure fast user lookups and attribute queries. Traditional LDAP-based directories struggle with query latency at large scale, leading to slow access control decisions. To improve performance, IAM solutions utilize graph databases (Neo4j, Amazon Neptune) for identity relationship mapping, key-value stores (Redis, etcd) for session caching, and high-performance indexing techniques to accelerate role-based access control (RBAC) and attribute-based access control (ABAC) policy evaluations.

IAM solutions serving millions of users must implement intelligent caching mechanisms to reduce authentication system load. By caching frequently accessed user attributes, session tokens, and authorization decisions, IAM platforms prevent excessive database queries and API calls. Distributed caching solutions such as Redis, Memcached, and AWS ElastiCache enable near-instant identity lookups, reducing backend processing overhead. Additionally, token introspection caching and JWT validation offloading optimize OAuth and OIDC authentication flows, ensuring that repeated access token verifications do not impact performance.

Authorization performance is a key challenge in large-scale IAM deployments. Traditional IAM systems rely on policy engines that evaluate access requests synchronously, causing delays when processing complex RBAC, ABAC, or policy-based access control (PBAC) rules. High-performance IAM solutions integrate Open Policy Agent (OPA) and eBPF-based policy evaluation mechanisms to accelerate dynamic access control decisions. By precompiling access policies, implementing hierarchical caching for authorization results, and parallelizing policy evaluations, IAM solutions reduce authorization response times to sub-millisecond levels.

Identity synchronization and provisioning at scale require event-driven processing architectures to ensure that IAM systems remain up-to-date with real-time identity changes, role assignments, and access revocations. Instead of batch-processing identity updates, high-performance IAM solutions use streaming data pipelines such as Apache Kafka, AWS Kinesis, and Google Pub/Sub to propagate identity events across distributed IAM components. By implementing event-driven IAM orchestration, organizations ensure that new user accounts, role modifications, and authentication policy changes are immediately reflected across all identity services.

High-scale IAM solutions must support multi-cloud and hybrid identity federations, ensuring seamless authentication and authorization across AWS, Azure, Google Cloud, and on-premises IAM systems. Instead of maintaining separate IAM configurations per cloud provider, organizations deploy federated identity brokers that unify authentication flows across multiple environments. By leveraging OIDC federation, trust-based SAML integrations, and Just-In-Time (JIT) identity provisioning, high-performance IAM architectures enable frictionless access across distributed enterprise infrastructures.

Security and compliance requirements become more complex as IAM systems scale. Large-scale IAM platforms must ensure continuous authentication monitoring, anomaly detection, and risk-aware identity governance. To detect and mitigate identity-based threats, high-performance IAM solutions integrate AI-driven behavioral analytics, identity threat intelligence, and machine learning-based anomaly detection. Security teams utilize real-time IAM security analytics powered by OpenTelemetry, Fluentd, and SIEM platforms (Splunk, ELK, Azure Sentinel) to correlate authentication events, detect privilege escalations, and prevent identity fraud at scale.

IAM systems handling millions of identities must also implement failover strategies, distributed authentication nodes, and disaster recovery architectures to ensure continuous uptime. Instead of relying on single-region deployments, high-performance IAM solutions deploy geo-distributed authentication clusters, active-active identity directories, and multi-region API gateways to prevent downtime and ensure authentication availability even during infrastructure failures. Load balancing techniques such as round-robin DNS, global traffic distribution (Cloudflare, AWS Route 53, Azure Traffic Manager), and service mesh-based authentication routing (Istio, Linkerd) further enhance IAM scalability and resilience.

Federated authentication and passwordless authentication strategies reduce the need for high-volume credential storage and password resets, minimizing IAM infrastructure load. By integrating FIDO2/WebAuthn, passkeys, and biometric authentication, high-performance IAM solutions eliminate password-based authentication overhead, ensuring faster, more secure, and scalable login experiences. Additionally, progressive identity proofing mechanisms, such as blockchain-backed verifiable credentials (VCs) and decentralized identifiers (DIDs), enhance scalability while reducing centralized identity verification bottlenecks.

Optimizing IAM APIs for high-throughput authentication and authorization requests is critical for large-scale deployments. High-performance IAM solutions implement GraphQL-based identity APIs, rate-limiting mechanisms, API gateway authentication caching, and gRPC-based low-latency authentication protocols to reduce authentication latency and maximize request concurrency. API-driven IAM services also leverage serverless authentication backends (AWS Lambda, Google Cloud Functions, Azure Functions) to scale IAM workloads dynamically based on real-time authentication demand.

By designing high-performance IAM solutions that incorporate distributed authentication architectures, caching optimizations, event-driven identity processing, and AI-powered threat detection, organizations can efficiently manage millions of identities while maintaining security, compliance, and user experience standards. These solutions enable scalable, resilient, and adaptive identity management, ensuring that IAM systems support the growing demands of modern digital ecosystems.

Optimizing IAM Token Performance: Redis, Memcached, and Token Caching Strategies

Identity and Access Management (IAM) systems rely heavily on tokens to manage authentication and authorization workflows. Tokens, such as JSON Web Tokens (JWTs) and OAuth 2.0 access tokens, provide stateless authentication mechanisms, enabling secure access to applications, APIs, and microservices. However, token validation and management at scale introduce performance bottlenecks, especially when handling millions of authentication requests per second. Optimizing token performance using Redis, Memcached, and token caching strategies ensures low-latency authentication, reduced database load, and scalable IAM infrastructure.

Token validation requires cryptographic verification, signature checking, and expiration enforcement, which can become computationally expensive when processed at high volumes. Traditional IAM systems rely on direct token validation against identity providers, but this approach introduces latency and scalability issues. Instead, organizations implement token caching strategies that store, index, and retrieve tokens efficiently from high-performance in-memory data stores such as Redis and Memcached.

Redis is a high-speed, in-memory key-value store that provides low-latency token caching, supporting IAM solutions with millisecond-level authentication response times. By storing validated access tokens, refresh tokens, and session identifiers in Redis, IAM systems eliminate redundant cryptographic validation overhead, significantly improving authentication throughput. Redis supports automatic eviction policies, ensuring that expired tokens are purged from memory, preventing unnecessary cache bloat and maintaining optimal performance.

Memcached is another lightweight caching solution optimized for token storage, high-speed lookups, and low-memory overhead. Unlike Redis, which provides advanced data structures, persistence, and replication, Memcached is ideal for ephemeral token caching, where authentication tokens require short-lived storage with ultra-fast retrieval. IAM systems use Memcached for session token caching, API rate-limiting tokens, and OAuth 2.0 access token lookups, ensuring that authentication workflows remain highly responsive and scalable.

One of the most effective token caching strategies is JWT signature verification caching, where IAM systems prevalidate JWTs and cache verified signature results to reduce cryptographic verification load. JWTs use asymmetric cryptographic signing (RS256, ES256, EdDSA), requiring public key lookups and signature validation during every authentication request. To improve performance, IAM systems cache public keys from identity providers (IdPs) and token signing certificates in Redis, preventing repeated API calls to external IdPs. By implementing JWT introspection caching, IAM solutions store decoded token claims, reducing repeated decoding operations and authorization latency.

Another key optimization technique is OAuth 2.0 token introspection caching, where IAM systems cache access token metadata and active session states. OAuth 2.0 tokens often require real-time introspection to verify token validity, expiration, and revocation status. Instead of querying authorization servers on every token request, IAM systems cache token metadata in Redis, reducing IAM server load and network overhead. Access tokens, refresh tokens, and OpenID Connect (OIDC) ID tokens can be stored as structured JSON objects in Redis, allowing efficient token lifecycle management.

Token expiration and eviction policies are critical for maintaining token cache integrity and security. IAM solutions enforce time-based token expiration caching, ensuring that access tokens are automatically purged from cache upon expiration. Redis supports TTL (time-to-live) settings for cached tokens, preventing the reuse of expired authentication credentials. Additionally, IAM systems implement Least Recently Used (LRU) cache eviction strategies, ensuring that active authentication tokens remain in cache while stale tokens are efficiently removed.

IAM microservices and API gateways also leverage distributed token caching to ensure consistent authentication performance across multi-region deployments. By replicating token caches across multiple Redis or Memcached nodes, IAM solutions achieve high availability, fault tolerance, and global authentication consistency. Cloud IAM platforms such as AWS Cognito, Azure AD B2C, and Google Cloud Identity integrate with Redis-based token caches, ensuring seamless authentication and token validation across distributed cloud environments.

To further optimize token caching, IAM systems implement hierarchical caching layers, where JWTs and OAuth tokens are first cached in fast-access memory stores (Redis/Memcached), then backed by persistent identity storage (PostgreSQL, MongoDB, or DynamoDB). This multi-tiered caching approach ensures that authentication requests prioritize low-latency cache retrieval while maintaining long-term token persistence for security audits and compliance tracking.

IAM systems utilizing GraphQL-based authentication APIs optimize token caching by batch-processing token lookups, reducing individual

API requests, and consolidating token verification checks. By implementing GraphQL query-level caching, IAM solutions minimize redundant authentication requests, improving token retrieval efficiency for high-volume authentication workloads.

For API security, rate-limiting tokens and API throttling mechanisms use token-based request tracking in Redis to prevent authentication abuse, credential stuffing attacks, and brute-force login attempts. IAM security teams configure Redis-based rate-limiting policies, ensuring that authentication tokens are temporarily blocked if excessive failed login attempts are detected. Additionally, serverless IAM platforms use Redis-based token caching to dynamically scale authentication workloads, ensuring consistent performance under peak traffic loads.

Token caching strategies also enhance Zero Trust security architectures, where authentication and authorization must be continuously validated. IAM systems implement short-lived token caching, ensuring that session tokens expire quickly and are refreshed dynamically based on real-time security telemetry. By integrating behavioral risk analysis with Redis-backed token caches, IAM solutions enforce adaptive authentication, preventing unauthorized access based on real-time threat intelligence and anomaly detection insights.

IAM token performance optimizations must also consider token invalidation workflows, ensuring that revoked or compromised tokens are immediately removed from cache. Security teams implement real-time token revocation mechanisms that synchronize token blacklists, invalidation lists, and session terminations across distributed token caches. Redis Pub/Sub messaging enables instant token revocation propagation, ensuring that compromised tokens are immediately rendered unusable.

For IAM platforms that support multi-factor authentication (MFA), caching strategies optimize MFA token validation and session persistence. Instead of repeatedly querying IAM databases for MFA challenge results, IAM solutions cache verified MFA session states in Redis, reducing authentication delays while maintaining strong security enforcement. MFA authentication workflows that leverage FIDO2/WebAuthn tokens use temporary Redis-backed session stores to securely validate hardware security key challenges and biometric authentication responses.

Optimizing IAM token performance using Redis, Memcached, and token caching strategies ensures low-latency authentication, reduced IAM server load, and scalable security enforcement. By implementing JWT signature caching, OAuth token introspection acceleration, distributed session storage, and hierarchical token caching layers, IAM solutions efficiently handle millions of authentication requests while maintaining high availability, security, and compliance. These optimizations enable scalable, resilient, and high-performance IAM architectures, ensuring seamless identity verification for modern digital ecosystems.

Extending IAM Solutions for IoT and Edge Computing Security

Identity and Access Management (IAM) solutions have traditionally focused on securing human identities, enforcing authentication policies, and managing role-based access control for enterprise applications. However, with the rapid expansion of the Internet of Things (IoT) and edge computing, IAM systems must extend beyond user authentication to manage device identities, machine-to-machine (M2M) communication, and decentralized edge security policies. The dynamic nature of IoT ecosystems, real-time data processing at the edge, and security threats targeting connected devices require an IAM framework that integrates device identity lifecycle management, distributed authentication, and zero-trust enforcement across heterogeneous networks.

IoT environments introduce a unique set of challenges for IAM systems. Unlike traditional IT infrastructure, IoT networks consist of thousands to millions of interconnected devices, sensors, and gateways, each requiring secure authentication and controlled access. Traditional IAM architectures that rely on centralized authentication directories, single sign-on (SSO), and session-based authentication are insufficient for IoT because devices operate in low-power environments, limited connectivity zones, and decentralized networks. IAM solutions must incorporate lightweight authentication protocols, certificate-based identities, and decentralized trust models to effectively manage IoT security at scale.

One of the core extensions of IAM for IoT is device identity and credential management. Unlike human users, IoT devices require immutable and cryptographically verifiable identities that ensure authenticity and prevent unauthorized access. IAM solutions integrate Public Key Infrastructure (PKI), hardware root of trust (RoT), and device identity attestation mechanisms to establish secure IoT authentication workflows. X.509 digital certificates, Trusted Platform Module (TPM) attestations, and Decentralized Identifiers (DIDs) are used to create tamper-resistant device identities that support secure authentication and authorization policies.

IAM for IoT must also support lightweight authentication mechanisms optimized for constrained environments. Traditional authentication protocols such as OAuth 2.0 and SAML introduce excessive computational overhead for resource-limited IoT devices. Instead, IAM solutions leverage OAuth 2.0 Device Authorization Grant, MQTT-based token exchanges, and CoAP security extensions (DTLS, OSCORE) to enable low-latency authentication in IoT environments. By implementing JWT-based device authentication with asymmetric cryptographic signing (EdDSA, ECDSA), IAM systems ensure that devices can securely authenticate without excessive processing requirements.

A fundamental extension of IAM for IoT security is zero-trust access control for edge computing. Unlike traditional IAM models that rely on network perimeter security, zero-trust IAM frameworks enforce continuous authentication and fine-grained access control for every IoT request, API call, and device interaction. IAM solutions integrate with edge identity gateways and policy decision points (PDPs) to dynamically evaluate device posture, security compliance, and anomaly detection insights before granting access to critical IoT resources.

Edge computing environments require decentralized identity governance, where IAM solutions operate across distributed IoT gateways, fog nodes, and cloud services. Instead of relying on a single identity provider (IdP), IAM systems integrate federated identity models, blockchain-based identity registries, and cross-domain trust mechanisms to ensure seamless authentication across IoT networks, industrial control systems (ICS), and smart infrastructure deployments. Federated IAM for IoT utilizes OIDC federations, OAuth 2.0 token sharing, and decentralized verifiable credentials (VCs) to enable secure cross-network authentication without exposing centralized authentication endpoints to potential attacks.

IAM solutions for IoT security must enforce dynamic risk-based authentication (RBA) to mitigate identity spoofing, rogue device infiltration, and compromised device takeovers. Unlike static authentication models, RBA continuously evaluates device behavior, access frequency, and geolocation context to determine whether additional verification is required. Machine learning-driven IAM analytics monitor device telemetry, network traffic patterns, and security compliance checks, enabling real-time risk scoring for IoT access requests. Devices exhibiting anomalous behavior, such as unexpected firmware modifications, abnormal API requests, or deviations from normal access patterns, trigger step-up authentication and access quarantining to prevent security breaches.

IAM for IoT and edge computing also requires strong authorization models that scale across dynamic device ecosystems. Traditional Role-Based Access Control (RBAC) is insufficient for IoT because device interactions are often context-dependent, event-driven, and require fine-grained access control policies. IAM solutions extend Attribute-Based Access Control (ABAC), Policy-Based Access Control (PBAC), and Relationship-Based Access Control (ReBAC) to enforce dynamic authorization policies based on device type, operational context, environmental conditions, and security posture assessments.

A critical component of extending IAM for IoT security is secure device onboarding and lifecycle management. Unlike user identities, which remain relatively stable, IoT devices experience frequent provisioning, decommissioning, and firmware updates, requiring IAM solutions to dynamically provision, authenticate, and revoke device credentials throughout the device lifecycle. IAM platforms integrate Zero-Touch Provisioning (ZTP), blockchain-based identity attestation, and Device Identity Access Management (DIAM) frameworks to ensure that only authorized devices can register and communicate within IoT ecosystems.

IAM security for IoT also extends into edge-to-cloud identity synchronization, ensuring that authentication, authorization, and identity governance policies remain consistent across edge nodes, cloud IAM services, and IoT gateways. IAM systems utilize distributed ledger-based identity synchronization, cryptographic key rotation policies, and time-sensitive token expiration mechanisms to prevent IoT identity fraud, man-in-the-middle attacks, and unauthorized device impersonation.

Threat detection and IAM security monitoring for IoT require real-time identity telemetry ingestion, anomaly detection pipelines, and threat intelligence integration. IAM solutions extend OpenTelemetry, Fluentd, and SIEM (Security Information and Event Management) platforms to collect IoT authentication logs, failed device login attempts, access control policy violations, and privilege escalation events across distributed IoT environments. Security teams use AI-driven IAM analytics and behavioral risk assessment models to identify compromised IoT devices, rogue network infiltrations, and policy-bypassing attempts before they escalate into security incidents.

Modern IAM solutions for IoT and edge computing also incorporate privacy-preserving authentication mechanisms, ensuring that sensitive identity attributes remain encrypted and decentralized. Privacy-enhancing IAM frameworks leverage Zero-Knowledge Proofs (ZKPs), Homomorphic Encryption, and Secure Multi-Party Computation (SMPC) to enable identity verification without exposing raw authentication credentials. This approach protects industrial IoT deployments, healthcare IoT ecosystems, and smart city infrastructures from identity-based cyber threats while maintaining compliance with global data privacy regulations (GDPR, CCPA, NIST 800-207).

Extending IAM for IoT and edge computing security requires scalable, resilient, and adaptive identity management frameworks that integrate lightweight device authentication, zero-trust access control, and machine learning-based risk assessment. By leveraging federated IoT identity models, decentralized identity attestation, and AI-driven threat detection, IAM solutions ensure secure, scalable, and policy-driven authentication across modern IoT and edge ecosystems.

Managing Identity Synchronization Across Disconnected Environments and Air-Gapped Networks

Identity synchronization is a critical challenge in environments where continuous connectivity is not guaranteed, such as air-gapped networks, remote military installations, classified data centers, and industrial control systems (ICS). Traditional IAM solutions rely on real-time directory synchronization, API-driven identity propagation, and cloud-based federated authentication, but these approaches fail in disconnected or restricted network environments. Organizations operating in high-security, mission-critical, and isolated environments must develop resilient identity synchronization strategies that ensure secure authentication, role consistency, and access control enforcement even in the absence of network connectivity.

Disconnected environments require offline-capable identity management architectures, where identity data, authentication mechanisms, and authorization policies are pre-synchronized, securely stored, and periodically updated. Unlike standard IAM deployments that depend on continuous cloud connectivity, air-gapped environments enforce strict network isolation, controlled data exchange policies, and manual synchronization workflows, requiring secure, cryptographically signed identity updates that cannot be tampered with during transmission.

One of the core approaches to managing identity synchronization in disconnected environments is the pre-staging and controlled replication of identity directories. Instead of relying on real-time Active Directory (AD) or LDAP synchronization, IAM systems must preload and securely distribute identity records, hashed credentials, role assignments, and group memberships to local directory servers or edge identity nodes. These identity repositories operate in isolation, ensuring that users can authenticate and access resources even when external connectivity is unavailable.

Secure identity replication workflows in air-gapped networks involve one-way, signed, and encrypted synchronization channels, ensuring that identity updates cannot be intercepted, modified, or corrupted. Organizations implement hardware-based data transfer mechanisms, cryptographic signing, and offline key validation to securely transfer identity updates, credential revocations, and access control policy changes into air-gapped systems. Hardware security modules (HSMs), Trusted Platform Modules (TPMs), and USB-based cryptographic tokens play a critical role in ensuring the integrity of offline identity data exchanges.

Authorization in disconnected environments requires offline-capable access control models, where IAM solutions precompute role-based access control (RBAC) and attribute-based access control (ABAC) decisions before deployment. Instead of relying on dynamic policy evaluation via centralized IAM services, organizations generate cryptographically signed access control lists (ACLs), pre-authorized role assignments, and cached policy decision responses that can be enforced without requiring real-time access to policy engines. These pre-signed access policies ensure that privilege escalation attacks and unauthorized access attempts are prevented even when connectivity is lost.

To maintain identity integrity and consistency across disconnected nodes, IAM solutions implement delayed identity reconciliation mechanisms, where incremental identity updates are securely transmitted, verified, and applied when networks become available. These updates include new user enrollments, password changes, role modifications, account terminations, and security policy adjustments. Organizations use secure data transport methods, such as physically controlled media transfers, encrypted offline storage, and air-gapped network tunnels, to ensure that identity synchronization updates remain tamper-proof and verifiable.

Authentication in air-gapped environments requires local authentication providers that function independently of centralized identity services. IAM solutions deploy local authentication nodes, PKI-based identity validation, and biometric authentication systems to enable users to authenticate securely without external identity verification dependencies. For example, smart cards, hardware authentication tokens (YubiKeys, PIV cards), and pre-issued one-time passwords (OTPs) allow users to access restricted environments without requiring direct communication with IAM directories or identity providers.

Multi-factor authentication (MFA) in disconnected networks must also be self-contained and resistant to network-dependent validation checks. Traditional MFA methods such as push notifications, SMS-based OTPs, or real-time token validation via cloud-based authentication services are ineffective in air-gapped networks. Instead, IAM solutions leverage TOTP-based (Time-Based One-Time Password) authentication, offline biometrics, and pre-issued cryptographic challenge-response authentication to ensure secure user verification without requiring internet access.

Role and permission auditing in disconnected IAM environments requires tamper-proof logging, immutable audit trails, and delayed security log synchronization. Since real-time security event monitoring is not feasible in air-gapped networks, IAM solutions must store authentication logs, access events, and policy enforcement records locally, ensuring that they can be synchronized and reviewed later when connectivity is restored. These audit logs must be digitally signed, encrypted, and verifiable, preventing unauthorized modification, log tampering, or privilege abuse attempts.

Secure identity synchronization mechanisms rely on delayed cryptographic trust verification, ensuring that identity updates received in disconnected environments originate from trusted IAM authorities. Organizations implement blockchain-based identity attestation, cryptographic signing chains, and zero-trust verification models to validate delayed identity updates, access policy modifications, and account lifecycle changes once network access is restored. Threshold signature schemes and multi-party identity attestation protocols further enhance security, ensuring that identity changes cannot be manipulated during synchronization intervals.

IAM solutions in mission-critical air-gapped networks, such as defense, aerospace, and national security systems, enforce offline revocation controls, ensuring that compromised identities, revoked credentials, and unauthorized access attempts are immediately mitigated even without real-time IAM connectivity. This is achieved through pre-issued revocation lists, digital certificate blacklists, and hardware-enforced access control policies, ensuring that users with revoked privileges cannot authenticate or access restricted resources even if synchronization with central IAM services is delayed.

For organizations operating in hybrid air-gapped and connected environments, IAM solutions must provide dual-mode authentication workflows, where users can authenticate both online and offline depending on network availability. These workflows integrate federated identity models, trust-based credential delegation, and delayed authentication response caching, ensuring that identity verification remains secure and functional regardless of network conditions.

Identity synchronization in air-gapped networks also benefits from AI-driven anomaly detection and forensic identity reconciliation, where IAM solutions analyze delayed authentication logs, access control deviations, and privilege escalation attempts once identity updates are applied. AI-driven IAM analytics detect suspicious access patterns, delayed attack execution attempts, and identity takeover strategies that may have occurred during disconnected operation periods, ensuring that security teams can mitigate potential threats post-synchronization.

Organizations managing IAM synchronization across disconnected environments and air-gapped networks must implement secure, resilient, and verifiable identity replication architectures that ensure authentication continuity, access policy enforcement, and zero-trust security principles without relying on constant network connectivity. By leveraging offline authentication mechanisms, cryptographic identity synchronization, and tamper-proof access control enforcement, IAM solutions enable secure identity operations even in the most restricted and high-security environments.

Implementing IAM for Industrial Control Systems (ICS) and Operational Technology (OT)

Identity and Access Management (IAM) plays a critical role in securing Industrial Control Systems (ICS) and Operational Technology (OT), which power essential infrastructure such as energy grids, manufacturing plants, water treatment facilities, and transportation networks. Unlike traditional IT environments, ICS and OT systems prioritize availability, reliability, and real-time operation over security, making them prime targets for cyber threats, insider threats, and unauthorized access. Implementing IAM in these environments requires a tailored approach that balances secure identity verification, access control enforcement, and operational continuity without disrupting industrial processes.

ICS and OT environments consist of Supervisory Control and Data Acquisition (SCADA) systems, Distributed Control Systems (DCS), and Programmable Logic Controllers (PLCs), which interact with human-machine interfaces (HMIs), sensors, actuators, and real-time monitoring dashboards. Traditional IAM models that rely on centralized authentication, role-based access control (RBAC), and cloud-based identity providers (IdPs) do not align with the unique constraints of ICS and OT systems. These environments demand air-gapped security models, decentralized identity governance, and strict least-privilege enforcement to prevent unauthorized access to critical infrastructure.

One of the fundamental challenges in implementing IAM for ICS and OT is managing human and machine identities in a segmented network environment. Unlike IT networks, which operate with standardized authentication protocols, ICS and OT networks often rely on legacy authentication mechanisms, hardcoded credentials, and static access control lists (ACLs). IAM solutions must integrate multi-factor authentication (MFA), passwordless authentication (FIDO2/WebAuthn), and hardware-backed authentication tokens (HSMs, TPMs, smart cards) to secure operator logins, remote maintenance sessions, and privileged access to industrial control interfaces.

ICS and OT environments often have legacy systems that lack native IAM integration, requiring proxy-based authentication, protocol translation layers, and secure identity gateways to enforce modern IAM policies. Organizations deploy jump servers, privileged session management (PSM) solutions, and identity-aware firewalls to mediate authentication requests, ensuring that only authenticated and authorized users can interact with SCADA systems, PLCs, and critical OT assets.

IAM for ICS and OT must enforce Zero Trust security principles, where every identity, device, and network request is continuously verified. Traditional perimeter-based security models are ineffective in ICS environments, as attackers can exploit lateral movement techniques to compromise OT assets. IAM solutions implement risk-based authentication (RBA), dynamic session monitoring, and behavior-based anomaly detection to prevent credential misuse, privilege escalation, and unauthorized remote access attempts.

One of the key IAM components in ICS and OT security is Privileged Access Management (PAM), which controls administrator access, remote vendor logins, and critical infrastructure maintenance sessions. PAM solutions enforce just-in-time (JIT) privileged access, session recording, and automatic credential rotation to minimize attack surfaces and insider threats. For example, instead of granting permanent administrator access to SCADA engineers, PAM dynamically provisions temporary access based on job roles, device health, and security compliance policies.

Machine identities in ICS and OT introduce additional IAM complexities, as automated control systems, industrial robots, and IoT-connected sensors require authentication and authorization to exchange data, execute commands, and trigger automated responses. Unlike human users, these machine identities operate autonomously, continuously, and often across air-gapped networks. IAM solutions integrate X.509 digital certificates, device identity attestation (TPM-based authentication), and decentralized identity frameworks (DID, verifiable credentials) to secure machine-to-machine (M2M) communication and API-based control system interactions.

ICS and OT IAM implementations must support role-based access control (RBAC), attribute-based access control (ABAC), and policy-based access control (PBAC) to enforce fine-grained security policies for different operator roles, automation workflows, and network segments. For example, an RBAC model ensures that plant operators can monitor industrial sensors but cannot modify PLC configurations, while an ABAC policy may enforce location-based restrictions on remote maintenance access. Dynamic policy evaluation enables IAM solutions to adapt access permissions in real time based on security posture, operational context, and detected anomalies.

ICS environments frequently rely on air-gapped networks and isolated control zones, requiring offline-capable IAM solutions that function without continuous connectivity to external identity providers. IAM implementations deploy local authentication nodes, encrypted identity synchronization mechanisms, and PKI-based authentication frameworks to ensure that authentication and access control policies remain enforceable even in disconnected ICS environments.

IAM solutions for ICS and OT also integrate with Security Information and Event Management (SIEM) platforms, Security Orchestration, Automation, and Response (SOAR) systems, and industrial anomaly detection engines to correlate authentication events with security threats, detect unauthorized access attempts, and automate incident response workflows. Organizations deploy OpenTelemetry-based IAM logging, real-time access policy auditing, and forensic session replay tools to investigate security incidents, detect credential abuse, and enforce regulatory compliance.

Regulatory compliance plays a critical role in ICS and OT IAM implementations, as industrial environments must adhere to NIST 800-82 (Industrial Control System Security), IEC 62443 (OT Cybersecurity Standard), and NERC CIP (Energy Grid Protection Standards). IAM solutions ensure compliance by automating identity governance, enforcing security baselines, and generating audit-ready access control reports that track who accessed what systems, when, and for what purpose.

To prevent identity-based threats in ICS and OT, IAM solutions enforce continuous monitoring, privileged session isolation, and real-time access policy enforcement. AI-driven behavioral analytics detect unusual operator activity, unauthorized configuration changes, and privilege escalation attempts, allowing security teams to block malicious access requests, revoke compromised credentials, and quarantine high-risk IAM sessions before they impact industrial operations.

Remote access security is a critical component of ICS IAM strategies, as third-party contractors, field technicians, and external vendors often require access to industrial systems for maintenance and support. IAM solutions implement secure remote access gateways, VPN-less authentication (Zero Trust Network Access), and role-scoped virtual desktop sessions to ensure that remote users only access pre-approved resources with time-limited permissions.

IAM for ICS and OT security extends beyond traditional user authentication to machine identity governance, policy-based automation, and air-gapped security enforcement. By integrating federated authentication, risk-based access controls, and AI-driven security analytics, IAM solutions provide scalable, resilient, and zero-trust security enforcement for industrial environments. These implementations ensure that critical infrastructure remains protected from cyber threats, insider attacks, and operational disruptions while maintaining continuous industrial uptime and regulatory compliance.

Secure Cross-Cloud IAM Implementations: Multi-Cloud Identity Federation

As enterprises increasingly adopt multi-cloud strategies, managing identity and access across AWS, Azure, Google Cloud, and private cloud environments has become a significant challenge. Traditional IAM models are designed for single-cloud or on-premises environments, making it difficult to enforce consistent authentication, authorization, and governance across multiple cloud platforms. Multi-cloud identity federation provides a framework for secure cross-cloud authentication, centralized identity governance, and dynamic access policy enforcement, ensuring that users and services can seamlessly authenticate across disparate cloud environments while maintaining strict security controls.

A core requirement of multi-cloud IAM is ensuring federated identity authentication, allowing users to sign in once using a central identity provider (IdP) and access services across multiple cloud platforms without requiring separate credentials for each cloud provider. Identity federation enables organizations to establish trust relationships between cloud IAM systems, enforce standardized authentication workflows, and minimize identity silos. By integrating OAuth 2.0, OpenID Connect (OIDC), and Security Assertion Markup Language (SAML), enterprises can authenticate users centrally while delegating access management to cloud-native IAM solutions.

Cloud-native IAM services, such as AWS IAM, Azure Active Directory (Azure AD), and Google Cloud IAM, provide built-in identity federation capabilities, allowing organizations to integrate existing enterprise identity systems with cloud authentication frameworks. Instead of managing separate user directories for each cloud provider, multi-cloud IAM architectures rely on federated identity brokering, where a single IdP (such as Okta, Ping Identity, or Microsoft Entra ID) issues authentication tokens that are trusted by multiple cloud IAM systems.

One of the primary challenges of multi-cloud identity federation is ensuring consistent role-based access control (RBAC) and policy enforcement across different cloud environments. Each cloud provider defines IAM roles, permission models, and policy syntax differently, requiring organizations to establish cross-cloud role mappings and standardized identity attributes. Attribute-Based Access Control (ABAC) provides a scalable approach to defining dynamic access policies, ensuring that users can authenticate across clouds while enforcing granular access restrictions based on user attributes, job functions, security context, and device compliance.

To prevent privilege escalation and cross-cloud identity compromise, IAM solutions implement Just-In-Time (JIT) access provisioning, ensuring that users and services receive temporary, least-privilege permissions only when needed. Instead of granting long-lived cloud IAM roles, JIT access models enforce time-bound authorization policies, automatically revoking access once a task is completed. Cloud-native Just-In-Time role assignment mechanisms, such as Google Cloud's IAM Conditions, AWS IAM session policies, and Azure AD Privileged Identity Management (PIM), allow organizations to dynamically enforce risk-based, least-privilege access controls across multiple cloud providers.

Multi-cloud authentication workflows require federated Single Sign-On (SSO) to streamline identity verification across cloud environments. Federated SSO allows users to log in once using a corporate identity provider (IdP) and gain access to AWS, Azure, and Google Cloud resources without repeated authentication challenges. Cloud IAM services integrate with OIDC and SAML-based identity federation, ensuring that authentication sessions remain secure, token-based, and context-aware.

One of the most critical security concerns in multi-cloud IAM implementations is identity synchronization and lifecycle management. Organizations must ensure that user provisioning, deprovisioning, and role assignments remain consistent across all cloud environments to prevent identity drift. Identity Governance and Administration (IGA) platforms, such as SailPoint, CyberArk, and Saviynt, provide automated cross-cloud identity synchronization, ensuring that identity lifecycle events (e.g., onboarding, job changes, access revocations) are replicated across AWS IAM, Azure AD, and Google Cloud IAM in real time.

Secure cross-cloud IAM also relies on multi-cloud API security and service identity management, ensuring that cloud workloads, microservices, and serverless functions authenticate securely across cloud boundaries. Instead of using static IAM credentials or hardcoded API keys, organizations implement workload identity federation, allowing cloud-native services to authenticate using short-lived tokens and cryptographically signed assertions. AWS IAM Roles Anywhere, Azure Managed Identities, and Google Cloud Workload Identity Federation provide secure, passwordless authentication for multi-cloud workloads, preventing credential leaks and cross-cloud identity compromises.

To enhance security monitoring in federated multi-cloud IAM environments, organizations integrate IAM logs, authentication telemetry, and privilege access events into Security Information and Event Management (SIEM) platforms such as Splunk, ELK, and Azure Sentinel. By aggregating identity-related logs from multiple cloud IAM services, security teams gain real-time visibility into authentication anomalies, privilege escalation attempts, and suspicious cross-cloud access patterns. AI-driven anomaly detection engines correlate multi-cloud IAM events, detect identity compromise attempts, and enforce adaptive access policies based on real-time risk scoring.

One of the major challenges in multi-cloud IAM is identity federation across hybrid environments, where on-premises Active Directory (AD), legacy IAM systems, and cloud-based identity providers must interoperate. Organizations deploy hybrid identity bridges, such as Azure AD Connect, AWS Directory Service, and Google Cloud Identity Synchronization, ensuring that on-premises user identities are seamlessly federated with cloud IAM systems. Cloud Access Security Brokers (CASBs) further enhance multi-cloud identity security, enforcing policy-based access controls, real-time identity governance, and cross-cloud data loss prevention (DLP).

Multi-cloud IAM implementations must also enforce Zero Trust identity security, ensuring that authentication and authorization decisions are continuously verified across all cloud environments. Risk-based authentication (RBA), step-up verification mechanisms, and context-aware access policies prevent cross-cloud session hijacking, lateral movement attacks, and identity federation abuse. Cloud-native identity threat detection platforms, such as AWS GuardDuty, Azure AD Identity Protection, and Google Cloud Security Command Center, provide real-time identity risk assessment, blocking suspicious authentication requests and enforcing adaptive IAM security policies.

Organizations implementing multi-cloud IAM architectures must establish governance frameworks and identity security baselines to ensure that IAM configurations, access controls, and federated authentication policies remain consistent across all cloud platforms. Cloud Security Posture Management (CSPM) tools, such as Prisma Cloud, AWS Security Hub, and Microsoft Defender for Cloud, provide automated IAM security posture assessments, misconfiguration detection, and identity compliance enforcement across multiple cloud environments.

To prevent vendor lock-in and IAM fragmentation, organizations adopt multi-cloud identity abstraction layers, allowing IAM policies to be centrally managed and dynamically enforced across cloud providers. Standardized identity schemas, identity broker proxies, and unified IAM policy engines (e.g., Open Policy Agent, HashiCorp Boundary, and SPIFFE/SPIRE) enable organizations to define consistent authentication and authorization policies across AWS, Azure, Google Cloud, and hybrid identity environments.

By implementing secure cross-cloud IAM architectures, enterprises ensure scalable, federated identity authentication, robust privilege management, and seamless multi-cloud access governance. Multi-cloud IAM federation enables flexible, secure, and policy-driven identity verification, ensuring that users, applications, and workloads authenticate securely across diverse cloud environments while maintaining strong security, compliance, and operational efficiency.

IAM and AI: Developing AI-Based Identity Verification and Access Controls

Artificial Intelligence (AI) is transforming Identity and Access Management (IAM) by introducing automated identity verification, adaptive access controls, behavioral analytics, and risk-based authentication mechanisms. Traditional IAM systems rely on rule-based policies, static authentication mechanisms, and predefined access control lists, which often fail to adapt dynamically to evolving security threats, insider risks, and identity fraud attempts. AI-powered IAM solutions leverage machine learning models, deep learning algorithms, and anomaly detection systems to enhance identity verification accuracy, enforce adaptive access policies, and prevent unauthorized access in real time.

One of the most critical applications of AI in IAM is intelligent identity verification, which improves the accuracy and reliability of user authentication, document validation, and biometric recognition. AI-driven identity proofing systems analyze facial recognition data, fingerprint scans, voice biometrics, and behavioral patterns to verify whether a user is legitimate before granting access. Neural networks and deep learning models improve identity verification accuracy by recognizing subtle facial feature variations, detecting deepfake attempts, and analyzing behavioral anomalies that may indicate synthetic identity fraud or impersonation attacks.

AI-based IAM solutions integrate with government databases, financial institutions, and decentralized identity platforms to cross-verify identity attributes, detect mismatches, and prevent identity theft. AI-powered identity proofing enhances Know Your Customer (KYC) and Anti-Money Laundering (AML) compliance by ensuring that users submitting identity documents are genuine and that their credentials match existing trusted records. These AI models analyze document authenticity, signature consistency, and photo alignment to prevent the use of forged or manipulated identity documents.

AI-driven risk-based authentication (RBA) is another key enhancement in IAM, allowing real-time assessment of authentication attempts based on behavioral risk factors. Traditional IAM systems enforce static MFA policies, requiring one-time passcodes (OTPs), security tokens, or biometric verification for every login attempt. AI-powered RBA solutions evaluate user behavior, geolocation, device reputation, login history, and contextual data to determine whether additional authentication is required. If AI models detect anomalous login behavior, device spoofing, or high-risk access requests, the system can trigger step-up authentication or block the attempt entirely.

Behavioral biometrics, powered by AI-driven identity analytics, further enhance IAM security by analyzing typing speed, mouse movements, touchscreen gestures, and navigation patterns to build unique user behavior profiles. If an authenticated session deviates from a previously learned user behavior model, AI-based IAM solutions flag the session as potentially compromised, requiring additional verification. These continuous authentication mechanisms reduce reliance on static login credentials, ensuring that identity validation is an ongoing process rather than a one-time event.

AI enhances real-time privilege management and dynamic access control enforcement, ensuring that users receive only the permissions they need based on risk context, job role, and security posture. Traditional Role-Based Access Control (RBAC) and Attribute-Based Access Control (ABAC) models often struggle with role explosion, privilege creep, and excessive permission assignments. AI-powered Policy-Based Access Control (PBAC) dynamically adjusts permissions based on real-time security telemetry, user behavior analytics, and AI-generated risk scores. AI-driven IAM systems can automatically downgrade, revoke, or grant privileges based on changing risk conditions, ensuring that excessive access rights do not persist over time.

AI-powered anomaly detection models enhance IAM security by identifying identity compromise attempts, session hijacking, and privilege escalation exploits. Traditional SIEM-based IAM monitoring relies on static correlation rules, which often miss advanced identity-based threats. AI-driven IAM analytics analyze massive volumes of authentication logs, access events, and privilege changes to detect subtle deviations in identity behavior that indicate potential security breaches. Machine learning models continuously refine anomaly detection baselines, reducing false positives while improving attack detection accuracy.

IAM automation powered by AI-driven identity governance streamlines user provisioning, deprovisioning, and access certification workflows. Traditional IAM governance processes require manual access reviews, periodic role audits, and administrator intervention to enforce identity lifecycle management. AI automates identity risk scoring, access entitlement recommendations, and privilege cleanup, ensuring that users only retain permissions necessary for their job functions. AI-driven IAM solutions detect orphaned accounts, enforce least-privilege access policies, and predict identity-related risks before they lead to security incidents.

AI enhances fraud detection and insider threat mitigation by analyzing historical IAM logs, access request patterns, and privilege escalation behavior to uncover malicious activity before it impacts the organization. AI-driven IAM systems can detect when an insider attempts to access unauthorized resources, bypass security controls, or escalate their own privileges. These models correlate cross-system identity interactions, flagging users who exhibit high-risk behavior across multiple cloud environments, applications, and privileged account systems.

In multi-cloud environments, AI-powered IAM orchestration ensures seamless identity synchronization, federated authentication, and cross-cloud access policy enforcement. AI-driven IAM platforms analyze access request patterns, role assignments, and security compliance violations across AWS IAM, Azure Active Directory, and Google Cloud IAM, ensuring that identity governance remains consistent across all cloud environments. AI models detect misconfigured IAM policies, unauthorized API token usage, and cloud privilege mismanagement, preventing identity sprawl and access control misalignment.

AI-driven IAM analytics integrate with Security Orchestration, Automation, and Response (SOAR) platforms, enabling real-time identity threat detection, automated response workflows, and incident remediation. If AI-based IAM systems detect a high-risk authentication event, compromised credentials, or unusual privilege changes, SOAR platforms can trigger automated response actions, such as revoking access tokens, resetting compromised credentials, or enforcing MFA revalidation. AI-powered IAM automation reduces incident response times and minimizes identity-related security risks.

AI-driven IAM compliance enforcement ensures that organizations remain aligned with GDPR, HIPAA, PCI-DSS, and NIST 800-63 by continuously monitoring access controls, identity authentication policies, and privileged account usage. AI models automatically flag IAM misconfigurations, detect non-compliant identity workflows, and generate real-time compliance reports, reducing manual auditing efforts and ensuring regulatory adherence. AI-based IAM governance enables proactive compliance enforcement, ensuring that security policies dynamically adjust to evolving regulatory requirements.

AI-enhanced zero-trust identity models ensure that IAM security remains adaptive, risk-aware, and continuously verified. Instead of relying on static authentication and access control mechanisms, AI-driven IAM solutions enforce context-aware authentication, real-time risk assessments, and identity trust scoring. AI-driven zero-trust architectures continuously validate identity claims, enforce behavioral-based access control, and dynamically adjust authentication requirements based on evolving security risks.

By integrating AI-driven identity verification, risk-based authentication, anomaly detection, and automated privilege management, IAM solutions evolve into self-learning, adaptive, and highly secure identity ecosystems. AI-powered IAM ensures stronger authentication, intelligent access governance, and proactive security enforcement, providing scalable, resilient, and future-proof identity security for modern digital enterprises.

Advanced IAM Resilience Strategies: Active-Active Architectures and Disaster Recovery Planning

Identity and Access Management (IAM) is a mission-critical component of enterprise security, ensuring that users, applications, and services authenticate securely and access resources based on well-defined policies. As organizations adopt multi-cloud, hybrid, and globally distributed architectures, IAM systems must maintain high availability, fault tolerance, and rapid failover capabilities to prevent authentication disruptions, access failures, and security breaches. Traditional IAM architectures, which rely on single-region deployments or active-passive failover strategies, introduce significant risks, including authentication bottlenecks, identity provider downtime, and latency-driven failures. To address these challenges, active-active IAM architectures and disaster recovery (DR) planning provide a robust framework for ensuring IAM resilience, business continuity, and security enforcement under all conditions.

Active-active IAM architectures are designed to ensure continuous availability, fault tolerance, and global redundancy by deploying IAM services across multiple data centers, cloud regions, or geographically distributed edge nodes. Unlike active-passive architectures, which require manual or delayed failover procedures, active-active IAM systems distribute authentication workloads dynamically across multiple identity providers, ensuring that no single point of failure can disrupt authentication workflows. These architectures integrate global load balancing, distributed session management, and multi-region identity synchronization to maintain a seamless, always-available authentication experience for users and applications.

One of the key components of active-active IAM is global traffic management (GTM), which intelligently routes authentication requests to the nearest or healthiest identity provider (IdP) node based on network latency, regional availability, and failover policies. IAM solutions deploy DNS-based load balancing (e.g., AWS Route 53, Azure Traffic Manager, Google Cloud Load Balancing) to direct authentication requests to active IAM instances across different cloud providers or data centers. If a regional IdP node becomes unavailable due to network failures, cloud outages, or security incidents, GTM automatically redirects authentication requests to healthy IAM nodes, ensuring continuous authentication availability.

IAM resilience strategies also incorporate distributed identity replication and real-time data synchronization to maintain consistent authentication states, access policies, and user session data across active-active deployments. Traditional IAM solutions often rely on monolithic database architectures, which create performance bottlenecks and single points of failure. In contrast, active-active IAM systems utilize distributed identity stores (e.g., AWS DynamoDB, Google Cloud Spanner, Apache Cassandra, or CockroachDB) to ensure that identity attributes, authentication logs, and session tokens remain synchronized across multiple regions.

Disaster recovery (DR) planning for IAM focuses on minimizing downtime, preventing authentication failures, and ensuring rapid identity system restoration following network outages, cyberattacks, natural disasters, or cloud service disruptions. Organizations must implement comprehensive IAM DR strategies, including automated failover mechanisms, immutable identity backups, and emergency access policies, to maintain business continuity during unexpected disruptions.

A critical component of IAM DR planning is automated failover orchestration, which ensures that identity services can recover instantly when primary IAM nodes experience failures. IAM disaster recovery playbooks integrate with orchestration platforms (e.g., Kubernetes, Terraform, Ansible) to automatically spin up standby IAM instances, restore identity session states, and reassign authentication traffic to functional identity nodes. These playbooks eliminate manual intervention delays, ensuring that identity authentication remains uninterrupted during DR scenarios.

IAM resilience strategies also leverage immutable backups and forensic identity recovery mechanisms to protect against data corruption, privilege escalation attacks, and identity database tampering. Unlike traditional IAM backups, which rely on scheduled snapshots that may become outdated, active-active IAM deployments implement real-time transaction logging, point-in-time recovery (PITR), and cryptographically signed identity audit trails to ensure secure, tamper-proof identity restoration. If an identity database becomes compromised or corrupted, organizations can roll back authentication states and access policies to the last known secure configuration, preventing identity-related security breaches.

High-availability IAM systems also enforce resilient authentication policies that remain functional even when primary IAM providers are unreachable. Federated identity caching, offline authentication tokens, and decentralized identity attestations ensure that users can continue authenticating and accessing resources even during widespread IAM outages. IAM solutions integrate edge-based authentication mechanisms, such as FIDO2/WebAuthn hardware keys and self-sovereign identity (SSI) models, to allow passwordless authentication that does not depend on central identity providers.

IAM disaster recovery planning must also consider privileged access resilience, ensuring that administrators, security teams, and critical system operators can regain access to IAM systems following major disruptions. Traditional IAM architectures often introduce single points of failure in privileged access workflows, where losing access to a primary identity provider prevents critical incident response and IAM restoration efforts. To mitigate this risk, organizations deploy break-glass emergency access policies, allowing pre-approved administrators to authenticate using time-restricted, encrypted emergency credentials that are stored securely in hardware security modules (HSMs), offline cryptographic vaults, or physical security tokens.

IAM security monitoring and anomaly detection are essential for proactive resilience planning, ensuring that organizations can detect and mitigate identity-related incidents before they lead to system-wide failures. Active-active IAM solutions integrate with SIEM (Security Information and Event Management) and SOAR (Security Orchestration, Automation, and Response) platforms to analyze authentication anomalies, detect unauthorized identity changes, and trigger automated incident response workflows. Machine learning-driven anomaly detection ensures that identity compromise attempts, session hijacking, and insider threats are identified and contained before they impact IAM availability.

Regulatory compliance and IAM resilience must align to ensure that organizations meet business continuity, cybersecurity, and data protection mandates. Regulations such as NIST 800-53, ISO 27001, GDPR, and PCI-DSS require organizations to implement IAM disaster recovery policies, high-availability identity governance, and secure failover architectures. IAM resilience frameworks integrate with Cloud Security Posture Management (CSPM) tools, providing continuous identity security assessments, real-time IAM misconfiguration detection, and compliance reporting.

Advanced IAM resilience strategies also address multi-cloud authentication continuity, ensuring that users can authenticate and access resources across AWS, Azure, Google Cloud, and private cloud environments even during cross-cloud identity provider outages. Multi-cloud IAM architectures deploy federated authentication failover mechanisms, where OIDC, OAuth 2.0, and SAML identity tokens remain valid across different cloud providers, preventing authentication disruptions during cloud service failures.

IAM resilience strategies must also consider ransomware and identity-based cyberattacks, where attackers attempt to disable authentication services, exfiltrate privileged credentials, or lock administrators out of IAM platforms. IAM security teams implement honeytoken-based deception techniques, identity-based attack simulations, and AI-driven identity fraud detection models to ensure that identity compromise attempts are identified, isolated, and mitigated in real time.

By implementing active-active IAM architectures, automated disaster recovery strategies, and high-availability authentication workflows, organizations ensure that IAM systems remain resilient, scalable, and secure, preventing authentication disruptions, access control failures, and identity-related security breaches. These IAM resilience frameworks enable enterprises to maintain continuous identity verification, adaptive security enforcement, and real-time authentication failover, ensuring that users, applications, and workloads remain securely authenticated under all operational conditions.

Microservices IAM Design Patterns: API Gateways, Service Mesh, and Identity Delegation

Modern applications increasingly adopt microservices architectures, where services are decomposed into independent, scalable, and loosely coupled components. This shift enables resilience, scalability, and rapid development, but it also introduces significant Identity and Access Management (IAM) challenges, including service-to-service authentication, API security, identity propagation, and fine-grained authorization enforcement. Traditional IAM models, designed for monolithic applications, fail to provide scalable identity governance in distributed microservices environments. To address these challenges, IAM solutions leverage API gateways, service mesh architectures, and identity delegation patterns to enforce secure authentication and authorization across microservices.

API gateways play a central role in IAM for microservices, acting as entry points for authentication, authorization, and identity propagation. Instead of embedding IAM logic within each microservice, API gateways centralize authentication, enforce security policies, and validate identity tokens before requests reach backend services. Gateways such as Kong, Apigee, AWS API Gateway, and Azure API Management integrate with IAM solutions to support OAuth 2.0,

OpenID Connect (OIDC), and JWT-based authentication mechanisms. API gateways verify access tokens, enforce role-based access control (RBAC), and route identity-aware API requests while offloading security responsibilities from individual microservices.

Service mesh architectures enhance microservices IAM by introducing decentralized identity enforcement, zero-trust authentication, and mutual TLS (mTLS) for service-to-service communication. Unlike API gateways, which handle external client authentication, service meshes such as Istio, Linkerd, and Consul enforce identity security policies at the service-to-service level, ensuring that internal microservices communicate securely with mutual authentication and encrypted traffic. Service mesh sidecars authenticate workloads, validate identity claims, and enforce fine-grained authorization policies using WebAssembly (WASM) and Open Policy Agent (OPA) integrations.

One of the key IAM challenges in microservices is service identity and workload authentication, ensuring that microservices can authenticate and authorize each other securely. Instead of using static API keys or hardcoded credentials, microservices leverage federated service identities, workload identity tokens, and dynamic secret rotation. Cloud-native identity federation solutions, such as AWS IAM Roles for Service Accounts (IRSA), Google Cloud Workload Identity, and Azure Managed Identities, enable microservices to authenticate using short-lived, automatically rotated credentials.

Identity delegation is a crucial IAM pattern in microservices architectures, enabling services to act on behalf of users while maintaining security and auditability. Instead of passing user credentials or long-lived access tokens between services, identity delegation leverages OAuth 2.0 delegation models, token exchange mechanisms, and signed assertions to securely propagate identity context across microservices. The OAuth 2.0 Token Exchange (RFC 8693) framework allows services to obtain delegated access tokens, ensuring that authorization remains traceable and aligned with user identity claims.

IAM security in microservices requires fine-grained authorization controls, preventing excessive privilege exposure and unauthorized access. Traditional Role-Based Access Control (RBAC) is insufficient for dynamic microservices environments, where access decisions must be based on real-time context, service attributes, and request parameters. Modern IAM implementations leverage Attribute-Based Access Control (ABAC), Policy-Based Access Control (PBAC), and Open Policy Agent (OPA) to enforce dynamic, context-aware access policies across microservices. ABAC policies evaluate user attributes, device trust scores, geolocation, and API scopes before granting or denying access.

Service-to-service IAM security in microservices also relies on mTLS authentication and identity-aware networking, ensuring that only trusted workloads can communicate with each other. Service mesh solutions automatically issue workload certificates, verify service identities, and encrypt traffic between microservices. By integrating mTLS with identity providers and certificate authorities (CAs), microservices prevent man-in-the-middle attacks, unauthorized API calls, and lateral movement threats.

Microservices IAM observability and logging play a critical role in security monitoring, identity anomaly detection, and forensic auditing. IAM solutions integrate with Security Information and Event Management (SIEM) platforms, distributed tracing tools, and identity analytics engines to capture authentication failures, token misuse, and unauthorized service access attempts. By correlating IAM logs with API request metadata, security teams detect identity compromise attempts, API abuse patterns, and privilege escalation attacks.

IAM resilience in microservices architectures requires redundant authentication workflows, failover identity providers, and token caching strategies. API gateways and service meshes implement JWT caching, OAuth token introspection acceleration, and adaptive identity failover mechanisms to ensure authentication remains uninterrupted during IAM outages. Distributed identity replication ensures that identity claims, access policies, and session states remain synchronized across multiple regions.

For microservices running in multi-cloud and hybrid environments, IAM architectures implement federated authentication models, cross-cloud identity synchronization, and decentralized trust management. Identity federation standards such as SAML, OIDC, and SPIFFE

(Secure Production Identity Framework for Everyone) allow microservices to authenticate across AWS, Azure, Google Cloud, and on-premises workloads without duplicating IAM policies.

Zero-trust IAM models in microservices enforce continuous authentication, just-in-time privilege escalation, and session re-evaluation based on real-time risk analysis and AI-driven anomaly detection. Instead of granting static long-term access permissions, IAM solutions dynamically adjust service privileges based on evolving security conditions, behavioral analytics, and compliance requirements.

By integrating API gateways, service mesh architectures, identity delegation, and fine-grained authorization models, IAM solutions enable scalable, resilient, and zero-trust identity enforcement in microservices environments. These IAM design patterns ensure that authentication, authorization, and identity security remain dynamic, policy-driven, and highly adaptive across modern cloud-native architectures.

Customizing Open Source IAM Solutions: Keycloak, WSO2, and Authelia Development

Open source Identity and Access Management (IAM) solutions provide a flexible, extensible, and cost-effective alternative to proprietary IAM platforms. Organizations seeking custom authentication, authorization, and identity federation often turn to Keycloak, WSO2 Identity Server, and Authelia to build tailored IAM solutions that align with their security and compliance requirements. These platforms offer pluggable authentication mechanisms, fine-grained access control policies, API-driven identity management, and integration with external identity providers (IdPs). However, customizing and extending these solutions requires deep technical knowledge of their architectures, plugin ecosystems, scripting languages, and policy engines.

Keycloak, an open-source IAM platform developed by Red Hat, is widely used for single sign-on (SSO), OAuth 2.0 and OpenID Connect (OIDC) authentication, and identity brokering. It provides a highly extensible architecture, allowing organizations to customize authentication flows, token issuance policies, and role-based access control (RBAC) models. Keycloak supports custom authentication providers, event listeners, identity federation, and SPI (Service Provider Interface) extensions, enabling organizations to integrate it with legacy authentication systems, external security tokens, and multi-factor authentication (MFA) mechanisms.

Customizing authentication workflows in Keycloak involves creating custom authentication providers and authenticators that modify the default login process. Organizations implement Java-based authentication modules to enforce custom MFA policies, adaptive authentication mechanisms, and device-based access restrictions. Keycloak's authentication SPI allows developers to define custom authentication steps, enforce password policies dynamically, and integrate risk-based authentication (RBA) logic based on geolocation, user behavior, or device health checks.

Extending Keycloak's identity federation capabilities enables seamless integration with external identity providers (IdPs) such as Azure Active Directory, Google Identity Platform, and custom LDAP directories. The platform provides federated identity mappers, allowing organizations to synchronize identity attributes, transform user claims, and enforce conditional access policies across multiple authentication sources. Custom identity providers (IdP plugins) in Keycloak extend OAuth2, OIDC, and SAML authentication, enabling support for non-standard authentication protocols and industry-specific identity federation models.

Keycloak's event listeners and custom actions enable real-time identity monitoring, authentication logging, and identity-based anomaly detection. Organizations implement custom event handlers to trigger security alerts, log authentication attempts, and enforce automated identity governance workflows. These event listeners are integrated with SIEM platforms (Splunk, ELK, Azure Sentinel) and identity analytics engines to provide real-time IAM security monitoring and compliance auditing.

WSO2 Identity Server (WSO2 IS) is another powerful open-source IAM solution, offering fine-grained access control, identity federation, multi-tenancy support, and API-driven IAM capabilities. Unlike Keycloak, which focuses on federated authentication and single sign-on, WSO2 IS provides XACML-based access control, Just-In-Time (JIT) user provisioning, and adaptive authentication policies. Customizing WSO2 IS requires understanding its extensibility framework, writing custom authentication handlers, and defining XACML-based policy enforcement rules.

Developers customizing WSO2 IS create custom identity connectors, authentication scripts, and federated login handlers to enforce dynamic role mapping, biometric authentication integration, and compliance-driven access control policies. WSO2's Adaptive Authentication Framework supports JavaScript-based policy enforcement, enabling organizations to implement conditional MFA, risk-aware authentication, and session-based identity scoring.

One of WSO2 IS's key customization features is extending Just-In-Time (JIT) user provisioning workflows, allowing organizations to dynamically map user attributes, enforce identity validation policies, and synchronize external identity directories. By customizing JIT provisioning handlers, organizations ensure that user accounts are created dynamically upon authentication, reducing the need for pre-provisioned identities in enterprise IAM systems.

WSO2 IS also enables policy-driven access control customization using XACML (eXtensible Access Control Markup Language). Organizations define custom attribute-based access control (ABAC) rules, ensuring that access decisions consider contextual attributes such as device trust, user risk score, and location-based restrictions. By extending WSO2's entitlement engine, IAM engineers create fine-grained access policies that enforce real-time authorization decisions across cloud applications, APIs, and microservices.

Authelia is a lightweight self-hosted identity provider designed for small to medium-scale IAM implementations, particularly in homelab, DevOps, and Kubernetes-based environments. Unlike Keycloak and WSO2, which focus on enterprise IAM use cases, Authelia provides a streamlined approach to authentication, MFA enforcement, and reverse proxy-based access control. Customizing Authelia involves modifying its authentication backend, defining policy-based authorization rules, and integrating with custom identity providers.

Organizations customizing Authelia develop custom authentication backends, integrating LDAP directories, SQL-based user stores, or external identity providers via OIDC. By modifying Authelia's configuration files and authentication schemas, organizations enforce custom user authentication logic, password hashing algorithms, and MFA challenge sequences.

Authelia's reverse proxy-based authentication model enables securing self-hosted applications, microservices, and DevOps pipelines using JWT-based authentication and fine-grained access control policies. By customizing Authelia's policy enforcement engine, organizations define custom security rules that restrict application access based on user groups, IP ranges, and risk-based conditions.

One of the most useful features of Authelia is its extensibility through webhooks and API-driven authentication flows. Organizations integrate custom webhook actions that trigger security alerts, automate identity workflows, and log authentication events into SIEM platforms or DevOps monitoring tools.

All three IAM solutions—Keycloak, WSO2 IS, and Authelia—support containerized deployments, Kubernetes orchestration, and multi-cloud IAM architectures. Organizations deploying these solutions in high-availability environments implement custom clustering configurations, database replication strategies, and active-active failover mechanisms to ensure fault tolerance and IAM service continuity.

Security customization in open-source IAM platforms also includes fine-tuning identity governance policies, securing admin APIs, and implementing cryptographic best practices. Organizations enhance IAM platform security by integrating hardware security modules (HSMs), enforcing OAuth2 token encryption, and implementing real-time identity anomaly detection using AI-driven security analytics.

By customizing Keycloak, WSO2, and Authelia, organizations extend authentication workflows, enforce custom access policies, and integrate IAM with existing enterprise security ecosystems. These open-source IAM platforms provide flexibility, extensibility, and security, enabling organizations to build scalable, policy-driven, and zero-trust IAM architectures tailored to their specific business, compliance, and security requirements.

IAM Code Security Best Practices: Static Code Analysis (SAST) and Dynamic Code Testing (DAST)

In the field of Identity and Access Management (IAM), ensuring the security of code is critical to protecting sensitive data and maintaining compliance with industry standards. Organizations that develop and manage IAM solutions must adopt robust security practices to detect and mitigate vulnerabilities before they can be exploited by malicious actors. Two key methodologies in securing IAM code are Static Application Security Testing (SAST) and Dynamic Application Security Testing (DAST). These techniques provide comprehensive security coverage by analyzing code both before and during execution, identifying weaknesses that could lead to security breaches. Implementing both SAST and DAST in IAM environments enhances the overall security posture and ensures that authentication, authorization, and access control mechanisms function securely.

SAST, often referred to as white-box testing, examines the source code, bytecode, or binary code of an application to detect security vulnerabilities early in the development lifecycle. This technique does not require the application to be running, allowing developers to identify and fix security flaws before deployment. SAST tools analyze the structure of the code to identify vulnerabilities such as SQL injection, cross-site scripting (XSS), buffer overflows, and hardcoded credentials. By integrating SAST into the continuous integration and continuous deployment (CI/CD) pipeline, developers can enforce security best practices at every stage of development, reducing the risk of releasing vulnerable IAM applications. One of the major benefits of SAST is its ability to provide immediate feedback to developers, enabling them to remediate issues before they become more costly and complex to fix. However, SAST has limitations, such as the potential for false positives, requiring security teams to validate findings before making code changes.

DAST, in contrast, is a black-box testing approach that evaluates an application while it is running. Unlike SAST, which focuses on the code itself, DAST simulates real-world attack scenarios to identify security vulnerabilities in the application's runtime environment. This technique is particularly useful for detecting vulnerabilities related to authentication mechanisms, session management, and input validation. DAST tools interact with the application just as an attacker would, sending requests to different endpoints and analyzing responses for security weaknesses. In IAM solutions, DAST helps uncover issues such as weak encryption, improper error handling, and inadequate protection of sensitive data in transit. One of the key advantages of DAST is its ability to identify runtime vulnerabilities that may not be evident through static analysis. However, DAST also has limitations, including the difficulty of achieving full code coverage and the potential for missing logic-based vulnerabilities that require a deep understanding of the application's internal structure.

Combining SAST and DAST in IAM security strategies provides a more holistic approach to application security. SAST allows developers to identify and fix vulnerabilities before deployment, while DAST helps uncover security flaws that manifest only when the application is running. By integrating both approaches, organizations can ensure that their IAM solutions remain secure against a wide range of threats. To achieve the best results, security teams should establish a secure software development lifecycle (SDLC) that incorporates both static and dynamic testing methodologies. This approach ensures that security is considered at every stage of development, from design and coding to testing and deployment. Automating security testing within CI/CD pipelines enhances efficiency and ensures that security checks are performed consistently across all development iterations.

In IAM environments, one of the critical aspects of security testing is verifying the robustness of authentication and authorization mechanisms. SAST tools help developers identify hardcoded credentials, insecure password storage, and improper privilege escalation, all of which could compromise user accounts. DAST, on the other hand, can simulate attacks such as brute force attempts, session hijacking, and token theft to evaluate how the IAM system responds under real-world conditions. These tests are essential for ensuring that authentication mechanisms do not contain vulnerabilities that could be exploited by attackers to gain unauthorized access. Additionally, IAM solutions must comply with security frameworks and regulations such as ISO 27001, NIST, and GDPR, making comprehensive security testing a fundamental requirement for achieving compliance.

Another important consideration when implementing SAST and DAST is the need for proper configuration and tuning of security testing tools. False positives and false negatives are common challenges in security testing, and without proper configuration, security teams may waste time investigating non-existent vulnerabilities or overlook critical threats. Organizations should customize SAST and DAST tools based on the specific requirements of their IAM applications, ensuring that they focus on detecting the most relevant threats. Regularly updating security testing rules and policies helps improve the accuracy of findings and ensures that emerging vulnerabilities are identified promptly.

Security testing in IAM is not a one-time activity but an ongoing process that requires continuous monitoring and improvement. As IAM solutions evolve and new features are introduced, security teams must reassess and refine their testing strategies to address emerging threats. Integrating security into the DevSecOps culture ensures that developers, security professionals, and operations teams work collaboratively to identify and remediate vulnerabilities in an efficient and timely manner. Security training for developers also plays a crucial role in enhancing the effectiveness of SAST and DAST by ensuring that code is written securely from the outset.

In addition to SAST and DAST, organizations can further strengthen IAM security by incorporating additional security measures such as software composition analysis (SCA), penetration testing, and runtime application self-protection (RASP). SCA tools help detect vulnerabilities in third-party libraries and dependencies, ensuring that open-source components do not introduce security risks. Penetration testing involves manual security assessments conducted by ethical hackers to identify weaknesses that automated tools might miss. RASP provides real-time protection by detecting and blocking attacks within the application's runtime environment, complementing the capabilities of SAST and DAST.

By adopting a multi-layered approach to security testing, organizations can enhance the security of their IAM solutions and reduce the risk of data breaches. Effective implementation of SAST and DAST enables security teams to proactively detect and mitigate vulnerabilities, ensuring that IAM applications provide strong protection against cyber threats. As attackers continue to evolve their tactics, organizations must remain vigilant and continuously improve their security testing methodologies to stay ahead of potential risks.

Building IAM Systems for Post-Quantum Cryptography and Future-Proofing Authentication

The rapid advancement of quantum computing poses significant challenges to modern cryptographic security, particularly in the field of Identity and Access Management (IAM). As quantum computers continue to evolve, traditional encryption algorithms that secure authentication processes and access control mechanisms may become vulnerable to quantum attacks. Organizations that rely on cryptographic protocols such as RSA, ECC, and Diffie-Hellman must begin the transition to post-quantum cryptography to ensure the long-term security of their IAM systems. Future-proofing authentication is a complex task that requires proactive planning, adaptation to emerging cryptographic standards, and a deep understanding of potential quantum threats. The integration of quantum-resistant algorithms into IAM infrastructures is essential for maintaining the integrity and confidentiality of sensitive data, preventing unauthorized access, and ensuring compliance with evolving security regulations.

One of the most significant risks posed by quantum computing is its ability to break widely used asymmetric encryption schemes.

Traditional public-key cryptography relies on mathematical problems that are computationally infeasible for classical computers to solve within a reasonable timeframe. However, Shor's algorithm, a quantum algorithm, enables quantum computers to efficiently factor large prime numbers, rendering RSA encryption obsolete. Similarly, elliptic curve cryptography (ECC), which is used extensively in IAM protocols, is also at risk because quantum algorithms can solve the discrete logarithm problem more efficiently than classical methods. These vulnerabilities create an urgent need for IAM systems to transition to post-quantum cryptography, which relies on mathematical problems that remain resistant to quantum attacks. Post-quantum cryptographic algorithms are designed to provide security even in the presence of powerful quantum computers, ensuring that authentication and access control mechanisms remain robust in the future.

Implementing post-quantum cryptography in IAM systems requires organizations to assess their existing cryptographic dependencies and identify components that rely on vulnerable encryption schemes. This process involves evaluating authentication protocols, digital signatures, secure key exchange mechanisms, and encrypted data storage systems. Many IAM frameworks currently depend on protocols such as TLS, which use RSA or ECC for secure communications. To future-proof authentication, organizations must adopt quantum-resistant cryptographic algorithms recommended by standardization bodies such as the National Institute of Standards and Technology (NIST). NIST has been leading an initiative to select and standardize post-quantum cryptographic algorithms that can replace vulnerable encryption methods. The adoption of these new algorithms will require updates to IAM software, authentication systems, and cryptographic libraries to ensure compatibility with quantum-resistant security mechanisms.

Another critical aspect of building IAM systems for post-quantum cryptography is ensuring backward compatibility and a smooth transition process. Many organizations operate in complex IT environments where legacy systems and modern cloud-based IAM solutions coexist. Replacing existing cryptographic protocols with post-quantum alternatives must be done carefully to avoid disruptions to authentication processes and access control policies. Hybrid cryptographic approaches provide a practical solution for transitioning to post-quantum security. These approaches involve implementing both classical and quantum-resistant encryption schemes in parallel, allowing IAM systems to maintain compatibility with existing infrastructures while gradually introducing post-quantum algorithms. This strategy ensures that organizations can transition to quantum-safe authentication without immediately abandoning legacy systems that rely on traditional cryptographic mechanisms.

Security teams must also consider the implications of post-quantum cryptography on user authentication methods, including password-based authentication, multi-factor authentication (MFA), and biometric authentication. Traditional authentication mechanisms often rely on cryptographic hashing and digital signatures for secure identity verification. Post-quantum cryptographic algorithms must be integrated into these authentication methods to maintain security in a quantum-threatened environment. Organizations should evaluate quantum-resistant alternatives for hashing functions and digital signatures, ensuring that they provide the necessary level of security while maintaining efficient authentication performance. Additionally, user authentication flows must be designed to support cryptographic agility, allowing IAM systems to switch to stronger encryption methods as new threats emerge.

The transition to post-quantum cryptography in IAM systems is not only a technical challenge but also a regulatory and compliance concern. Many industries, including finance, healthcare, and government sectors, operate under strict security regulations that mandate the use of strong encryption to protect sensitive data. As quantum computing progresses, regulatory bodies are expected to update security standards to reflect the need for quantum-resistant encryption. Organizations must stay informed about these regulatory changes and ensure that their IAM systems comply with new security requirements. This may involve updating cryptographic policies, conducting risk assessments, and implementing security controls that align with post-quantum cryptographic best practices.

Future-proofing authentication also requires a shift in IAM architecture towards more flexible and resilient security frameworks. Zero Trust security models, which emphasize continuous verification and least privilege access, can play a crucial role in mitigating quantum threats. By implementing Zero Trust principles, organizations can reduce their reliance on traditional cryptographic authentication methods and adopt more adaptive security mechanisms. This approach involves verifying user identities at multiple layers, using context-aware authentication, and employing behavioral analytics to detect anomalies. Post-quantum cryptography can be integrated into Zero Trust architectures to enhance the overall security of IAM systems, ensuring that authentication mechanisms remain robust against evolving threats.

The development of post-quantum cryptography also presents challenges in terms of performance and scalability. Quantum-resistant algorithms often require larger key sizes and more computational resources than their classical counterparts. This can impact the efficiency of IAM systems, particularly in environments that handle high volumes of authentication requests. Organizations must carefully evaluate the performance implications of post-quantum cryptographic algorithms and optimize their IAM architectures to support secure and efficient authentication. This may involve leveraging hardware acceleration, optimizing cryptographic implementations, and utilizing distributed authentication models to balance security and performance requirements.

As the adoption of quantum computing increases, threat actors may attempt to exploit cryptographic vulnerabilities before organizations have fully transitioned to post-quantum security. A potential risk is the "harvest now, decrypt later" attack strategy, in which attackers intercept and store encrypted data with the intent of decrypting it once quantum computers become powerful enough. To mitigate this risk, organizations must prioritize the adoption of quantum-resistant encryption for protecting sensitive data, ensuring that authentication credentials, session tokens, and access control information remain secure even in the face of future quantum advancements. Implementing forward secrecy in IAM protocols can further reduce the risk of retrospective decryption by ensuring that encryption keys are regularly updated and not reused over extended periods.

Preparing IAM systems for post-quantum cryptography is a long-term endeavor that requires collaboration across the cybersecurity industry. Researchers, cryptographers, and technology vendors must work together to develop, test, and standardize quantum-resistant authentication mechanisms. Organizations should actively participate in industry discussions, contribute to post-quantum security research, and collaborate with IAM solution providers to ensure that their authentication infrastructures remain secure against emerging threats. By adopting a proactive approach, organizations can safeguard their IAM systems from the disruptive impact of quantum computing, ensuring that authentication and access control mechanisms remain resilient in the years to come.

Developing IAM Solutions for Regulatory Compliance in Finance, Healthcare, and Government

Identity and Access Management (IAM) plays a critical role in ensuring security, privacy, and compliance with regulatory requirements in industries that handle sensitive data, such as finance, healthcare, and government. These sectors are subject to strict regulations designed to protect personal information, prevent fraud, and maintain the integrity of digital identities. Organizations operating in these industries must implement IAM solutions that not only enhance security but also align with legal and regulatory frameworks. Developing IAM systems for compliance requires a comprehensive approach that includes secure authentication, access control, audit logging, and continuous monitoring to meet industry-specific regulatory standards. A well-designed IAM framework must be able to enforce role-based access control (RBAC), least privilege principles, and multi-factor authentication (MFA) while ensuring transparency and accountability in identity governance.

The financial sector is heavily regulated to prevent identity theft, money laundering, and unauthorized access to sensitive financial information. Regulations such as the General Data Protection Regulation (GDPR), the Sarbanes-Oxley Act (SOX), and the Payment Card Industry Data Security Standard (PCI DSS) impose strict security requirements on financial institutions. IAM solutions in finance must enforce strong authentication mechanisms to protect customer accounts and prevent fraudulent transactions. Implementing MFA is a critical requirement, ensuring that financial services are safeguarded against credential theft and phishing attacks. Additionally, IAM systems must support risk-based authentication, which evaluates contextual factors such as location, device type, and behavioral patterns to determine whether additional verification is required before granting access. Secure API management is another important aspect of IAM in finance, as financial institutions increasingly rely on open banking initiatives that require controlled access to banking services. Ensuring that APIs are protected with OAuth 2.0 and OpenID Connect standards is essential for maintaining compliance and preventing unauthorized data access.

In the healthcare industry, IAM solutions must comply with regulations that protect patient data and ensure secure access to electronic health records (EHRs). The Health Insurance Portability and Accountability Act (HIPAA) in the United States mandates strict access controls to protect patient confidentiality, while the European Union's GDPR enforces similar privacy protections. Healthcare IAM systems must provide granular access controls to restrict access to patient records based on roles and responsibilities. For example, a nurse should only have access to patient data relevant to their department, while a specialist should only access records necessary for treatment. Role-based and attribute-based access control (ABAC) models help healthcare organizations enforce these restrictions effectively. Another key requirement in healthcare IAM is audit logging and monitoring, as regulations require organizations to track and report all access to sensitive patient information. IAM solutions must generate detailed audit logs that record user activities, access requests, and authentication events to ensure compliance with regulatory reporting requirements. Single Sign-On (SSO) solutions can also improve security and efficiency in healthcare environments by allowing healthcare professionals to access multiple systems with a single set of credentials while maintaining regulatory compliance.

Government agencies face unique challenges in IAM compliance due to the vast amount of sensitive and classified data they manage. Regulations such as the Federal Information Security Management Act (FISMA) in the United States and the European Union's Network and

Information Security (NIS) Directive require government institutions to implement strict security measures to protect public sector data. IAM solutions for government organizations must provide high levels of identity assurance and authentication strength to prevent unauthorized access to classified information. Implementing identity proofing mechanisms, such as biometric authentication and hardware security keys, helps strengthen access security for government employees and contractors. Zero Trust security models, which assume that no user or device should be trusted by default, are increasingly adopted in government IAM implementations to mitigate insider threats and external cyberattacks. Access to government databases and systems must be continuously verified based on risk assessments, device health, and behavioral analytics to prevent unauthorized access to sensitive data.

Regulatory compliance in IAM requires organizations to implement strict identity governance and administration (IGA) processes to enforce policies, manage user roles, and ensure access reviews are conducted regularly. Automated provisioning and de-provisioning of user accounts are essential to reducing security risks associated with orphaned accounts and excessive privileges. Compliance frameworks such as the National Institute of Standards and Technology (NIST) Cybersecurity Framework and the International Organization for Standardization (ISO) 27001 emphasize the importance of continuous identity lifecycle management to prevent security vulnerabilities related to outdated or unauthorized user access. Organizations must also implement privileged access management (PAM) solutions to protect administrative accounts that have elevated access to critical systems. PAM tools enforce just-in-time access policies, requiring privileged users to request temporary access rather than maintaining persistent administrative privileges, thereby reducing the risk of insider threats and credential compromise.

Encryption plays a crucial role in IAM compliance by ensuring that sensitive user credentials and authentication data are protected both in transit and at rest. Financial institutions must implement strong encryption standards such as Advanced Encryption Standard (AES) and Transport Layer Security (TLS) to protect customer authentication data from interception and tampering. Healthcare organizations must encrypt patient records to comply with HIPAA's security requirements and prevent unauthorized disclosure of medical information. Government agencies require encryption mechanisms that meet the highest security standards, including quantum-resistant cryptographic algorithms, to safeguard classified data from emerging cyber threats. Secure key management practices, such as using hardware security modules (HSMs) and implementing key rotation policies, further enhance IAM security and compliance by preventing unauthorized decryption of sensitive information.

Continuous compliance monitoring is essential to ensure that IAM solutions remain aligned with regulatory requirements as security threats and legal frameworks evolve. Organizations must implement security information and event management (SIEM) systems that integrate with IAM platforms to detect anomalies and potential compliance violations in real-time. Machine learning-based anomaly detection can enhance IAM security by identifying suspicious authentication attempts, insider threats, and credential stuffing attacks. Regulatory audits and penetration testing should be conducted periodically to validate IAM controls and ensure that authentication mechanisms remain resilient against cyber threats. Organizations must also establish incident response plans that define procedures for handling security breaches and regulatory violations, ensuring that compliance risks are mitigated effectively.

Developing IAM solutions for regulatory compliance requires a proactive and adaptive approach that balances security, usability, and legal requirements. Organizations in finance, healthcare, and government must continuously evaluate and update their IAM frameworks to address emerging security challenges while maintaining compliance with evolving regulations. Collaboration between security teams, legal experts, and compliance officers is essential to designing IAM solutions that meet industry standards while providing seamless and secure access to critical systems and data.

Scaling IAM for Billions of Requests: Rate Limiting, Load Balancing, and High Availability

Identity and Access Management (IAM) systems play a crucial role in securing digital identities and enforcing access control policies across large-scale applications and distributed environments. As organizations expand their digital footprint, IAM solutions must be capable of handling billions of authentication and authorization requests without compromising security, performance, or availability. Modern enterprises, cloud service providers, and large-scale platforms process vast amounts of identity-related traffic, requiring IAM architectures that can efficiently scale while maintaining reliability. Scaling IAM systems to support billions of requests involves a combination of rate limiting, load balancing, and high availability strategies, ensuring that authentication and authorization services remain resilient under extreme workloads.

One of the key challenges in scaling IAM systems is managing the sheer volume of authentication requests without overloading the infrastructure. Authentication services, particularly those supporting single sign-on (SSO), multi-factor authentication (MFA), and federated identity providers, must handle peak loads efficiently to prevent service disruptions. Rate limiting is an essential mechanism for controlling traffic, preventing abuse, and ensuring fair resource allocation. By implementing rate limiting, IAM systems can enforce policies that restrict the number of authentication attempts per user, IP address, or API client within a defined timeframe. This helps mitigate brute force attacks, credential stuffing attempts, and denial-of-service (DoS) attacks targeting authentication endpoints. Adaptive rate limiting mechanisms can dynamically adjust thresholds based on traffic patterns, identifying anomalous behavior and enforcing stricter limits when necessary. Combining rate limiting with risk-based authentication further enhances security by requiring additional verification steps for requests that exhibit suspicious behavior, such as rapid login attempts from multiple locations.

Load balancing is another critical component of scaling IAM systems to handle billions of requests efficiently. Authentication and authorization services must distribute incoming traffic across multiple servers, data centers, or cloud regions to prevent bottlenecks and ensure optimal performance. Load balancers play a crucial role in directing authentication requests to the least busy IAM nodes, reducing response times and preventing server overload. Organizations deploying IAM solutions at scale often utilize a combination of Layer 4 (transport-level) and Layer 7 (application-level) load balancing strategies to optimize request distribution. Layer 4 load balancing, which operates at the network transport level, enables efficient routing of authentication requests based on TCP and UDP connections. Layer 7 load balancing, on the other hand, operates at the application layer and allows IAM systems to route requests based on HTTP headers, cookies, and authentication parameters. This level of granularity enables more intelligent request distribution, ensuring that authentication requests requiring additional processing—such as biometric authentication or hardware token verification—are handled by appropriately resourced servers.

Ensuring high availability is paramount when scaling IAM solutions to support billions of requests. Downtime in IAM services can lead to widespread access disruptions, preventing users from logging into critical applications and causing cascading failures across dependent systems. High availability architectures incorporate redundancy, failover mechanisms, and geographically distributed deployments to maintain continuous service availability. IAM systems deployed in multi-region or multi-cloud environments leverage global traffic management solutions to route authentication requests to the nearest or healthiest IAM instance, minimizing latency and improving user experience. Active-active IAM deployments, where multiple instances operate simultaneously across different regions, provide seamless failover in the event of regional outages. To further enhance availability, organizations implement automated failover strategies that detect service disruptions and reroute authentication requests to backup instances without user intervention.

Scalability challenges in IAM extend beyond handling high request volumes; they also include managing session persistence, token lifetimes, and distributed caching. IAM systems generate authentication tokens, session IDs, and access credentials that must be validated efficiently across a distributed infrastructure. Session persistence mechanisms, such as sticky sessions or distributed session storage, help maintain consistency when authentication requests are processed by multiple IAM nodes. However, relying on a single session store can introduce performance bottlenecks, making distributed caching a critical component of scalable IAM solutions. In-memory data stores such as Redis and Memcached enable fast lookup and validation of authentication tokens, reducing the load on backend authentication servers. Organizations implementing OAuth 2.0 and OpenID Connect protocols must optimize token issuance and validation workflows to prevent unnecessary processing overhead. Token expiration policies and refresh token strategies must be carefully designed to balance security and performance while minimizing unnecessary re-authentication requests.

API gateways play a significant role in scaling IAM by acting as intermediaries between clients and authentication services. API gateways enforce rate limits, provide caching mechanisms, and distribute authentication requests efficiently across backend IAM components. By offloading authentication-related processing to API gateways, organizations can reduce the direct load on IAM servers and improve overall system performance. Integrating IAM with content delivery networks (CDNs) further enhances scalability by caching authentication responses and reducing the number of requests reaching origin servers. This approach is particularly effective in scenarios where IAM is used to authenticate users accessing web applications, as it minimizes authentication latency and improves responsiveness.

Another critical factor in scaling IAM is ensuring compliance with security and regulatory requirements while managing billions of authentication requests. Large-scale IAM deployments must adhere to industry standards such as GDPR, NIST, and ISO 27001, which mandate secure authentication practices, logging, and access controls. IAM systems must generate detailed audit logs for authentication events, including successful logins, failed authentication attempts, and access requests. Logging and monitoring solutions must be capable of handling high log volumes while providing real-time threat detection and anomaly identification. Security Information and Event

Management (SIEM) platforms and machine learning-based analytics help organizations detect patterns indicative of credential theft, insider threats, or automated attack attempts.

As IAM solutions scale, automation becomes a necessity for maintaining operational efficiency. Organizations must automate IAM provisioning, policy enforcement, and incident response workflows to reduce manual intervention and ensure consistent security enforcement. Infrastructure-as-Code (IaC) practices enable IAM components to be deployed and managed programmatically, allowing for rapid scaling and configuration updates. IAM policy automation, driven by machine learning algorithms, can dynamically adjust access control rules based on real-time risk assessments, ensuring that users receive appropriate access without unnecessary friction.

Scaling IAM for billions of requests requires a multi-layered approach that incorporates rate limiting to control traffic, load balancing to distribute requests, and high availability strategies to ensure continuous service operation. Organizations must optimize authentication workflows, leverage caching and API gateways, and implement compliance-driven security measures to maintain a resilient IAM infrastructure. As digital ecosystems continue to grow, IAM scalability will remain a key challenge, requiring constant innovation and adaptation to meet the demands of modern applications and user environments.

Becoming an IAM Architect: Moving Beyond Engineering into Enterprise Security Leadership

Transitioning from an Identity and Access Management (IAM) engineer to an IAM architect represents a significant shift in both technical expertise and strategic responsibility. While engineering roles focus primarily on implementation, troubleshooting, and system maintenance, the role of an IAM architect extends beyond coding and configuration into the broader domain of enterprise security leadership. This transition requires a deep understanding of security frameworks, risk management, governance, compliance, and business strategy. IAM architects serve as the bridge between technical teams and executive stakeholders, ensuring that identity security aligns with the organization's long-term goals while mitigating security threats and compliance risks.

Becoming an IAM architect begins with mastering the technical foundations of IAM, including authentication protocols, authorization models, identity federation, privileged access management, and directory services. A strong grasp of standards such as OAuth 2.0, OpenID Connect, SAML, and SCIM is essential, as these protocols govern identity flows across enterprise systems and cloud environments. Beyond technical knowledge, an IAM architect must develop an architectural mindset that prioritizes scalability, resilience, and security by design. This requires the ability to design IAM solutions that integrate seamlessly with existing enterprise systems while accommodating future growth and evolving security threats. Architects must think beyond immediate technical fixes and focus on creating sustainable identity frameworks that support the organization's digital transformation initiatives.

Strategic thinking is a core competency for IAM architects, as they must align IAM strategies with business objectives and security policies. Unlike engineers who primarily execute technical tasks, architects are responsible for defining the vision for IAM within the organization. This involves collaborating with IT leadership, CISOs, compliance officers, and business unit leaders to establish identity governance policies, streamline access management processes, and ensure regulatory compliance. IAM architects must articulate the value of identity security to non-technical stakeholders, demonstrating how IAM frameworks contribute to risk reduction, operational efficiency, and user experience improvements. Effective communication skills are essential, as architects must translate complex security concepts into actionable business recommendations that drive investment in identity security initiatives.

A critical aspect of the IAM architect role is designing identity security architectures that support Zero Trust principles. As organizations move away from traditional perimeter-based security models, IAM architects must develop access control strategies that enforce continuous verification, least privilege access, and adaptive authentication mechanisms. This requires implementing identity-centric security measures such as risk-based authentication, identity threat detection, and Just-In-Time (JIT) access provisioning. Additionally, architects must address the growing challenges of cloud IAM by designing multi-cloud and hybrid identity solutions that provide seamless and secure access across diverse IT environments.

Regulatory compliance is another major area of responsibility for IAM architects. Financial institutions, healthcare providers, government agencies, and enterprises operating in highly regulated industries must comply with security standards such as GDPR, HIPAA, PCI DSS, and SOX. IAM architects play a key role in ensuring that identity governance frameworks meet these compliance requirements by implementing role-based access control (RBAC), access certifications, privileged access controls, and audit logging. They must work closely with compliance teams to develop policies that align with industry regulations while ensuring that IAM solutions provide sufficient visibility and control over user access activities.

Leadership and influence are essential skills for IAM architects, as they must guide teams and influence security decisions at the enterprise level. Unlike engineers who work within defined technical scopes, architects are responsible for setting IAM standards, driving cross-functional collaboration, and advocating for security best practices across the organization. This requires the ability to manage stakeholder expectations, negotiate security priorities, and gain executive buy-in for IAM investments. Strong leadership skills enable IAM architects to mentor engineering teams, establish IAM governance committees, and foster a security-first culture within the organization.

The transition to an IAM architect role also requires continuous learning and professional development. Identity security is a rapidly evolving field, with emerging technologies such as passwordless authentication, decentralized identity, and post-quantum cryptography reshaping the IAM landscape. Architects must stay informed about industry trends, participate in cybersecurity forums, and obtain relevant certifications such as Certified Information

Systems Security Professional (CISSP), Certified Identity and Access Manager (CIAM), and Certified Information Security Manager (CISM). By staying ahead of technological advancements and regulatory changes, IAM architects ensure that their organizations remain resilient against evolving cyber threats.

IAM architects must also develop expertise in integrating IAM solutions with modern security architectures such as Security Information and Event Management (SIEM), Extended Detection and Response (XDR), and cloud security frameworks. Identity security is increasingly interconnected with broader cybersecurity initiatives, requiring architects to collaborate with security operations teams to detect and respond to identity-related threats. Integrating IAM with threat intelligence platforms and behavioral analytics tools enables proactive identity risk management, helping organizations detect compromised credentials, insider threats, and anomalous access patterns.

Another key responsibility of IAM architects is designing IAM automation and orchestration workflows to improve efficiency and security. Manual access provisioning and identity lifecycle management processes are prone to errors and inefficiencies, making automation a priority for modern IAM programs. By leveraging identity orchestration platforms, IAM architects can automate user onboarding, enforce policy-driven access controls, and implement self-service identity management capabilities. Automating IAM operations reduces administrative overhead, improves user experience, and enhances security by ensuring that access permissions are granted and revoked based on real-time risk assessments.

IAM architects must also focus on identity scalability, ensuring that IAM solutions can support the growing demands of enterprise users, partners, and customers. Large organizations process billions of authentication and authorization requests daily, requiring architectures that support high availability, load balancing, and performance optimization. Architects must design IAM infrastructures that can handle peak authentication loads without compromising security or user experience. This involves implementing distributed identity architectures, leveraging cloud-based IAM services, and optimizing directory synchronization mechanisms to support large-scale identity operations.

The shift from IAM engineering to IAM architecture represents a significant evolution in both technical depth and strategic impact. While engineers focus on implementing identity solutions, architects take a broader perspective, shaping the future of IAM within the enterprise. By mastering identity security principles, developing leadership skills, and aligning IAM strategies with business objectives, IAM architects play a vital role in securing digital identities, enabling compliance, and driving enterprise security innovation. As identity security becomes increasingly central to cybersecurity strategies, IAM architects will continue to be at the forefront of securing access to critical systems and data in an evolving threat landscape.